Reflections on a Dying Life

Donald X. Burt, O.S.A.

D1473050

LITURGICAL PRESS
Collegeville, Minnesota

www.litpress.org

1   2   3   4   5   6   7   8

Library of Congress Cataloging-in-Publication Data

Burt, Donald X.
    Reflections on a dying life / Donald X. Burt.
      p. cm.
    Includes bibliographical references.
    ISBN 0-8146-3017-0 (pbk. : alk. paper)
    1. Death—Religious aspects—Catholic Church. 2. Burt, Donald X. I. Title.

BT825.B94 2004
236'.1—dc22

2004009915

Contents

Introduction

We are now travelers on a journey. We cannot stay in this place forever. We are on our way, not yet home. Our present state is one of hopeful anticipation, not yet unending enjoyment. We must run without laziness or respite so that we may at last arrive at our destination. (*Sermon 103*, 1)

—

Some years ago when I was chaplain at a small New England college, I gave a sermon that began "Today the doctors have told me that I am going to die." Unfortunately (but happily, because it showed that I was loved), my announcement caused consternation. I was, after all, only thirty years old with a freshly minted Ph.D. in philosophy with a lifetime to pursue wisdom! I was too young to die! (or so they thought) Now, in my eighth decade with my philosophy career behind me (forty-four years of pursuing wisdom was quite enough), I am not sure that the reaction would be the same. Now, saying "I am going to die" might only prompt the response, "Has anybody claimed your T.V. yet?" Sad to say, when you reach "geezerhood" announcing your coming death may (if you are still loved) cause regret but little surprise.

The point of my announcement when I was still a "cool mover and shaker" (or so I thought) was simply that all of us are going to die someday, the only issue not resolved is when and how. This is not an extraordinary revelation for anyone who is a realist. St. Augustine in the fifth century was making this point over and over again in his sermons and conversations. His message was quite simple:

All of us are moving towards death. Indeed, we begin to die the moment we are conceived because we are put on a road that can lead nowhere else.

Perhaps this is the reason why T.S. Eliot wrote:

The whole earth is our hospital
Endowed by the ruined millionaire. (*Four Quartets: East Coker*, Ib)

We may feel like agreeing with Eliot on our bad days, days when we feel that the whole human race is in the same boat . . . and it is a hospital ship. We prove daily the truth of Augustine's observation that we have all been put into the furnace and have come out half-cracked (*Commentary on Psalm 99*, 11). Still, despite our cracks, most of us feel pretty good on some days at least. In any case we can't blame God for the days when we feel bad, the days when we mess up our lives and the lives of others. God is more than a "millionaire" and the wealth with which he endowed this life is all good. We are the ones who "ruined" it.

Though the place of our life just now is far from being a hospital, there is some truth in calling it a hospice. The *Oxford English Dictionary* defines "hospice" as a place where travelers find rest and entertainment and we are certainly travelers. We are on the road to eternity, and we could use some peace and entertainment as we make our way forward. I for one am comforted by seeing my life as being in an "Inn for Travelers," something like that "Inn of the Samaritan" referred to in Sacred Scripture (Luke 10:30-37). I like this description because my memory of the wayside inns of my traveling days is mostly pleasant. Far from being gloomy, they were bright and cheery. When I stayed there I understood that someday I had to leave, but my eventual leaving did not sour my satisfaction with my pleasing (though temporary) surroundings.

I remember especially one inn in the town of Cape Ann, Massachusetts. It was high on a cliff overlooking the Atlantic Ocean. The air was always fresh, the sky was often blue, and the scent of the sea saturated the land. Those who stayed there found it to be a fine place for relaxation, a quiet place for doing business, a bright place for having lunch with friends, a romantic place for making love.

The staff was geared to the clientele. They knew we who stopped by would soon be moving on, but as long as we stayed they dedicated themselves to making us as comfortable and happy as possible. If we did not feel too good on some days, they would do all they could to make our pain go away or at least help us endure it. When we felt just fine, they were quick to come and rejoice with us.

We travelers were in a "dying life" in a sense. The day would certainly come when we had to move on, a day when we had to "die" to our "inn experience." When that day for exiting came, those same good people who helped us live and laugh happily on the brink of the infinite sea, now came to our assistance in our leaving. They carried our bags, helped us figure out what we owed, and charged the bill against our account. As we left, they stood at the door waving goodbye, sad that we were leaving but happy that our travels were over and pleased that they had been able to help us on our way. They had made our whole life by the sea and our leaving easier to bear by being with us and caring for us and caring about us. Through their love they had supported us through all the days of our traveling life.

My life then and now is truly *in transit*, and so it is for all of us. Whether we are now feeling the pleasure of a good life or the pain of a bad life, whether we are in the innocence of our infant life or in the regrets of a life lived long but not always well, whether we are at the peak of our mental and physical powers, or at a stage where we are beginning to forget that "long ago" period when we were "flourishing" and not simply existing—in sum, whatever our condition is at the present moment, we are in the midst of a life that is moving towards death. We are in the midst of a truly *dying life*. Whether we are young or old, we are all travelers on the same road, a road that leads ultimately through the door of death to a life without death. We are in the midst of a life that is rushing towards that death-door that is the entrance to eternal life.

Our reason and experience tell us that we are moving towards death; our Christian faith tells us that we are moving ultimately to unending life. But to move from life to LIFE we must pass through death and as long as we live on this side of death, we need the comfort and support of others. We need their companionship and care through all the times of our life, both the bad and the good. If our times are bad, we need the concern of others to make them seem less bad. If they are good, we need the companionship of others to make them seem even better. As Augustine wrote long ago: "It is not easy to laugh when you are alone" (*Confessions*, 2.9.17).

The Christian faith assures us that whatever happens to us in this life, we will never be left alone. If we are lucky (and sadly some are not), we will always have some humans who care for us and who are willing to rejoice with us on our good days and support us on our days that are not so good. But even when we lose all of these, we will still have present with us a loving God—a God who, though unwilling to overrule the bad human decisions that cause so much of the suffering in life, has through his own death guaranteed that we can have perfect happiness on the other side of the door of death, and who in the meantime has promised that he will stay with us, supporting us along the way.

In the following pages (with the help of St. Augustine and some others) I offer reflections on our life now, our future death, and the life that awaits us thereafter. It will be organized under three headings:

Part 1: Life in the Inn for Travelers
Part 2: Death: The Door to Life
Part 3: Life After Death

Hopefully, these reflections will help me (and perhaps you) live nobly and happily during our remaining days in this hospice, this mostly pleasant place for travelers—those living out their days of a still dying life.*

---

*Unless otherwise indicated, all quotations are from the works of St. Augustine. Further reflections on the thought of Augustine can be found on my website: www41.homepage.villanova.edu/donald.burt.

| PART ONE |

LIFE IN THE INN
FOR TRAVELERS

We live here for a few days and then must move on. In this life we are no more than temporary boarders; only in heaven will we dwell in our own home. A sign that we are only visitors here is that someday we will hear the voice of the Lord commanding us: "Move On!" No one will tell us to "move on" once we are in our eternal home in heaven. Just now we can be nothing but wanderers. As the psalmist declares: "I am but a wayfarer before you, / a pilgrim like all my fathers" (Psalm 39:13).

As long as we live on earth our lodgings will not be permanent. Only when we get to that great land beyond death will the Lord give us dwelling places that abide. This is what he promised when he said: "There are many permanent abodes in my Father's house" (John 14:2).

Such eternal dwellings obviously cannot be reserved for mere lodgers but only for those who deserve to live there forever (*Commentary on Psalm 60, #6*).

A Flowing Life

As a torrent gathers together from the rains and overflows, roars, runs and by running hastens down until it finally finishes its course, so it is with our mortal life. The human race is collected together from hidden sources and flows on, and at death travels again to hidden places. This intermediate state that is life roars and passes away. (*Commentary on Psalm 109, 20*)

———

Life moves on through our various times and in our various places. We cannot hold on to either of these. We cannot stay in one place for all time. We cannot capture any one time in our life and make it last forever. The only stability in this ever-moving life is from those who travel with us . . . friends, lovers, and anyone who cares for us and about us . . . those who can share our various times and be with us in our various places.

Experiencing this flowing life is something like being in a movie theater. Our little self sits quietly in the darkness as the panorama of places and times passes by on the screen. The theater empties and fills again, new people arrive to be with us as the life on the screen passes by. Hopefully some nearby will not remain anonymous in the darkness but become friends and even lovers. If most eventually leave, we hope that new friends and lovers will join us in seeing the new times and places that are ever-flowing before and around us.

Watching an amusement park by the seashore and hearing the screams and cries of those thrown about on the various rides, the thought struck me that "no one screams on a ferris wheel." The pleasure comes from being in motion while yet staying in place. You go up and down, gently circling and recircling over the same place, creating the impression that all is stable and you are safe in the midst of your predictable movement.

The screaming comes from the other rides where the movement is rapid with many jerks and sways—sometimes upside down, sometimes right side up. There is an apparent danger because the motion seems out of control and unpredictable. You cannot know what is coming next. It seems that we can only be excited by motion. No one screams standing still watching the rides of others. We need motion to feel alive, but we want it to be controlled and held firmly in one place.

The paradox (or fallacy) of the ferris wheel making its gentle rounds in place is that it is rooted in an earth which is spinning and twisting at immense speeds through a dark space, whirling around a dangerous sun which would destroy it if it came too close. Moreover, this earth and this sun are themselves a minor part of an immense galaxy which itself is speeding off towards an unknown destiny.

Whether we like it or not, all reality is in motion, all life is flowing. We try to hold our lives still in their good times and pleasing places, but it cannot happen. We are speeding towards death where time will cease, the body will dissolve, and the spirit will begin to exist quietly in "no place" as it waits for the beginning of eternity. In the midst of our active moving life, we dream of the time when we can retire and enjoy peaceful stability in the place that we have built for ourselves. We forget that no time or place in this life can ever be forever.

There is a natural anxiety that comes with living in such a moving life. We desire happiness above all, to be alive and have meaning and find love and experience a freedom that allows us to control our environment. We become convinced that these great goods can only be achieved by finding a comfortable place which is forever, a place where we are surrounded by accustomed toys, a stable way of life and (most importantly) some who seem to care for us.

The fact of the matter is that we cannot be happy, indeed, we cannot live without change. Biologically, the process of life (metabolism) is created by a constant "building up" (anabolism) and "breaking down" (catabolism). Despite our efforts to hold onto that "perfect" condition of the body (whenever that was) through various creams and nostrums

> . . . the body that one has just now never remains the same. It does not stand still. It is changed as we grow in age; it is changed as we move from place to place. It is changed by changing times and by gradual deterioration. (*Commentary on Psalm 121*, #6)

It is good that such changes happen. Our bodies quickly tire of sameness. If we sit too long, we become stiff. If we stand too long, we become tired. If we lay in our bed too long, we develop sores. "Feeling good" demands motion, and we feel sorry for our poor friends who are paralyzed in place.

Our spirit also lives by changing. It is fine to think as a child when we are a child, but if we are ever to grow we must put aside childish thinking and begin to think as an adult. Our mental and spiritual life must grow if it is not to stagnate. As Augustine wrote to a friend:

> It is not true to say that a thing rightly done once should not be changed. Obviously, right reason demands a change in what was right to do at some earlier time if the time and circumstances change. (*Letter 138*, 1.4)

Of course, Augustine is not saying that there are no unchanging moral absolutes. The rule to "Love God above all and our neighbor as ourselves" is true in time and eternity. It is never good to "pretend to be God" or to claim to be "more human" than others. What he *IS* saying is that with changing times and circumstances, the way in which we express our love will and must change.

Nature itself dictates that I must change as I grow in age. Now a senior citizen, it would kill me to exercise as I did in my twenties. It would be silly to try to act like a teenager, much less to think as I once did when overwhelmed by puberty. Indeed, the very happiness of human life is found in the movement from age to age and the movement from the acting and thinking of earlier times. Boredom comes from sameness. It is only through the various changes in our lives that we bring excitement into life. To stay in one place too long leads to ennui. Anticipation of the "new," of being able to move on, brings joy. Indeed, Augustine believed that it is the very variety of life that gives it its beauty and makes us desire it (*The Nature of the Good,* #8).

Yet, having said all this, the flow of life can be frightening, especially when we realize that eventually it will end in death. The source of our hope must be in that one unchanging element in this moving universe: the presence of Christ. As Augustine says, he is like a tree on the shore of this raging river, a tree that we can reach out for and grasp as we plummet on (*Commentary on the First Epistle of John,* 2.10.2; see Psalm 1:3; Jeremiah 17:8).

One thing is sure. Like it or not, we are on the move and we need someone to care for us as we travel on our way. It is no fun to be in an Inn for Travelers by yourself. That is why I have given up traveling alone. It is too much of a burden and depressing to go to see new places without someone you love and who loves you. With them in your arms, even old places seem new. They reveal new ways in which your two lives and hearts can come together. Even when things are going badly, you have the consolation of hearing them whisper to you: "Do not be afraid! I will stay with you till journey's end."

Homeless at Villanova

A short time ago I was forced to move out of the home where I had lived for twenty-two years. The decision was made to renovate the Villanova Monastery and some sixty-one of us were forced to go elsewhere. I don't expect much sympathy. Certainly the disruption caused by my move cannot be compared to the suffering of refugees in foreign lands or to the conditions faced daily by the homeless in our cities. Still the move was upsetting, even though I had moved eighteen times over the last fifty-five years. (Join the Augustinians and see the world.) Probably this last move was distressing because I had assumed that I would stay at Villanova until I was carried off to spend my eternity "overlooking" the town of Conshohocken from the Augustinian burial plot high on the hill.

Luckily I was not sick when the command came to move (many of my confreres were not so lucky). It is especially hard to move when you get old and sick. My brother and his wife spent over thirty years in a nice house in the suburbs. There they raised their family and lived to see their grandchildren. But then the kids moved on, and my brother's dear wife died and he was alone in the big house with only his memories. However, the house contained good memories, and he was able to stay there peacefully for a few years more. But then he got sick, and it was necessary to move him into a nursing home. It was a good facility and the staff (especially one nurse) were very kind to him. The family and I visited frequently, but it was only to visit. He felt badly when we rose to leave because he could no longer go home with us. Later on, when he became a bit confused, he frequently asked to go home, but the home he spoke of was not the suburban house where he had spent thirty years. It was the old house in the city where he had spent his childhood. A few months later he died, finding the only permanent home that awaits any of us.

The truth of the matter is that for any of us to think that any "place" in this life is forever is a mistake. We are all living in a Hospice, an Inn for Travelers, and no room can be reserved for eternity. But knowing this does not take away anxiety. In my own case I had gotten comfortable with my surroundings. I believed I would spend my "reclining" years in peaceful meditation rather than having to move boxes.

Perhaps my recent move was worse than the others because I was now a "geezer" and retired from my old teaching job of forty-four years. Moving to a new job, a new task, a new challenge is exciting when you are young. When there is no new task to do, when you are called upon to move once again but now into a nursing home or some such facility, there is no longer excitement, only sadness. The call to move tells you that you have migrated from the wonderful days of "independent loving" to the days of "assisted living" where others are needed to keep your old engine running and your "lurching" progress on safe paths. You have run out of gas and are going nowhere. You are no longer "doing"; you are just "being," and others determine where and how you shall "be" until you "be no longer." At such a time "to be no longer" in this life can become very appealing. A grave is somewhat confining, but at least you are no longer aware of it. Shedding life when life seems worn out is like shedding old clothes: the size of the "dumpster" causes no pain.

In some ways we humans are much like those mangrove trees common along the Florida coastal marshes. In its search for stability, the mangrove drops tendrils into the changing tides to form new roots until the parent resembles a thicket more than an individual tree. These new roots gradually build up silt from the moving waters until at last the tree is able to embrace its own little piece of earth. In the midst of the ever-moving waters of the salt marsh, the proud tree has formed its own little island where it thinks that it will stand safe and secure above the rushing waters. In fact, its life depends on being washed by the moving tides. If it were ever lifted out of the swirling waters, it would lose its source of nourishment and quickly die.

We imitate the mangrove in trying to establish roots that will insure us a place of stability amidst the ebb and flow of the life around us. In search of such a safe haven, we try to surround ourselves with new "shoots" that are much like us, forming communities of like-minded people who share our history. In such a protective thicket we are happy, saying to ourselves: "Now I will be safe! Now I have roots that will secure my life forever!"

Of course, it is pure nonsense. We are still in the midst of the flow of time, and it is impossible to raise ourselves above its ever-moving tides. Whatever else happens to us in this life, we must face that ultimate "pulling up of roots" that is our death. Perhaps that is why we fear change so much. We pretend to be sturdy mangroves, but in fact we are more like feathery dandelion seeds, those delicate creations called "wushys" by young ladies of my acquaintance since it only takes a "wush" of one's breath to send them off to distant lands. We, like those air-borne seeds, are destined to float on the winds through life until finally we put down our roots in eternity. Until that happens, all the things, the honors, the places, the people we experience in this life are just passing events in an ever-moving world. To those who do not realize this, Augustine declares: "You are no better than foolish beasts. Indeed, you have become one of them" (*Commentary on Psalm 48/2*, 11).

Sometimes as we live out our days in this Hospice, we begin to suspect this. A feeling of "rootlessness" overcomes us.

We begin to realize that we are not at home, that we are on the road, and that someday we must leave. We pretend that this is not so. We try to convince ourselves that this little room that we have right now will be ours till the end of time, or, at least till the end of *our* time. But then our lives are disrupted in one way or another. We are asked to change rooms, to move out, to go to a new place in the Inn, to give up the kind Hospice care we have gotten used to in our "old homestead," to move on to a new place where we are not sure that anyone will care about us.

Of course, there are many folks who have never had and never will have a permanent home in this Inn. They have no room of their own but must exist in the corridors of the world, begging for a bit of food from passing crowds returning from dining. These are the truly homeless. But even the most settled in the Inn, even the ones with the most grand rooms, must someday move on. Like it or not, they are as "homeless" in the Hospice as their most unsettled neighbors. The transient nature of life is a condition that we must deal with, first by helping the truly homeless to have a decent life here on earth, and then by being ready to move on ourselves when the call comes for us to give up our customary and accustomed existence to move on to a new place.

To have no place to call your own is a lonely existence for the homeless, but lonely also are those who live in mansions but have no one there to be with them, to care about them, to care for them. They may have a house but they have yet to find a home.

"It's a Beautiful World!"

One of the things that makes us so reluctant to leave this world, this Hospice where we now reside, is its overpowering beauty. Seeing the beauty in this little space where we live out our lives, we begin to wonder if there is anything beyond our space and time that can equal it. We have found a beautiful heaven on earth and wonder if there is an even more beautiful heaven somewhere beyond the doors of this earthly Inn. Overcome with the beauty of our surroundings, we are loath to leave; indeed, we sometimes forget that someday we must leave.

But what is it that makes a sunset, an approaching storm, the one we love so beautiful and therefore pleasurable? Over the years those who have studied this question have concluded that our pleasure comes from seeing the *"perfection"* (that is, the unified wholeness) of the beautiful object, the *harmony* among its various parts and (above all) its clarity or *brilliance*.

Augustine believed that these qualities flowed from three fundamental properties of every existing thing:

Measure: which imposes the proper limit on every creature.

Number: which gives it a unique form, the specific qualities that make it to be *this* and not something other.

Weight: which pulls every creature to its proper state of repose and stability where it and all its parts are in their proper place. (*A Literal Commentary on Genesis,* 4.3.7)

These three characteristics combine to give to reality a "clarity" or "brilliance" which in many ways is the identifying trait of all that is beautiful. It was this "brilliance" that caused Jacob to choose Rachel over Leah as his wife (Gen 29:17). Poor Leah had no "sparkle" in her eyes while Rachel was "shapely and beautiful." Both were good women but Rachel had a *brilliance* which gave her a special beauty. Augustine suggests that poor Leah, like her namesake the "cow," had eyes deadened by the drudgery of everyday life whereas Rachel had the brightness of her namesake, the new-born "ewe-lamb," a new creation seeing for the first time the wonders of this world (*Against Faustus the Manichean*, 22.52).

Augustine was enchanted by the beauty of the world and some of his descriptions are almost poetic. For example, in the *City of God* he writes:

> Just think of the world in which we live! Think of the thousands of beautiful things for seeing and the thousands of materials just right for making things. There is an infinitely changing beauty in the sky and the land and the sea. What varieties of color do we see in the changing moon and sun and stars! There are the soft shadows of noon forests, the shades and smells of spring flowers, the different songs and exotic dresses of the birds. How amazing are the animals who surround us, the smallest ant even more amazing than the huge bulk of the whale! Think of the grand spectacle of the sea as it clothes itself in different colors, sometimes green, sometimes purple, sometimes the bluest of blue. And how grand it is when there is a storm (especially grand when you are not sailing on the heaving surface of the sea but are caressed by its soft mist as you stand safe and warm on the shore). (*City of God*, 22.24)

He believed that everywhere we look in nature we can see the beautiful order implanted in it by the hands of the Creator. It can be found in the reproductive power of the seed and in the song of the nightingale (*On True Religion*, 42.79), in tiny ants and bees as well as great animals (*Letter 137*, 2.8). Even the lowly worm is not without its special attractiveness, its pleasing roundness, the ordered fitness of all its parts from front to rear (*On True Religion*, 41.77).

Like the world of nature, human beings are beautiful because of the "measure, number, and weight" we discover in their outward appearance and inner character. There is no question that often our first attraction to others is through externals, their quiet talk, their gentle appearance, their well-formed body. As Augustine wrote:

> Quite apart from its practical usefulness, there is in the human body such a rhythm, poise, symmetry, and beauty that it hard to decide whether it was its usefulness or its beauty that the Creator had most in mind. (*City of God*, 22.24.4)

At the same time, we cannot know the "real person" if all we know are their externals. We may "see" them but we don't "know" them until we know something about what is happening inside them. As Augustine wrote to his friend Consentius: "Some whom we can see clearly with our eyes are undesirable and in fact scarcely endurable until the beauty of their interior spirit manifests itself by some outward sign" (*Letter 205*, 1). We may be first attracted to a beautiful woman or a handsome man by externals, but their allure quickly dissipates once we discover that their proper "measure, number, and weight" is only in their body. They may have the proper "limits" in their physique (being neither too large nor too small), but if their spirit has "delusions of grandeur" we are repelled. They may have all of the physical characteristics (the "number" or "form") of a human being, but if they are defective internally (for example, in not having the loving spirit expected of a social animal), we are not likely to embrace them. Finally, if internally they are "lightweights," happily finding their "place" in living the life of a hog, we turn away from them as being well-formed but empty shells.

The beauty of the body may attract us but it is only the beauty of the spirit that can enthrall us. This beauty of spirit is found in the moral integrity or virtue whereby they recognize their place in the universe and act accordingly (*Commentary on Psalm 44,* 29). It is this "virtue" that gives beauty to their spirit no matter how "deformed" their external appearance may be (*A Literal Commentary on Genesis,* 7.6.9). The beauty that comes from the virtuous integrity of a person's life is rooted in various noble qualities. First, the person accepts their *"limits."* They act their age; they accept their weaknesses; they recognize their strengths. Second, they know their *"number"* as human beings and avoid the temptations to act like beasts or pretend to be gods. Finally, they are gifted with the appropriate *weight* that draws them to love and seek their proper place in the universe. They seek the peace and tranquility of living an ordered life as a human being because that is what they are: neither more nor less.

The reason why we do not appreciate the beautiful things all around us (and in us) is that they have become too commonplace. Day after day we trample under foot miracles that, if understood, would fill us with awe (*Letter 137,* 3.10). We call some things "ugly" because our focus is too narrow, not seeing how the most humble part of the universe contributes to its total beauty. Even the color black is beautiful when seen in the context of the multi-colored picture of which it is a part (*On True Religion,* 40.76). Certainly all in nature is passing away, but in the very passing away of its parts and the coming to be of replacements there is a great beauty (*A Literal Commentary on Genesis,* 1.8.14). Deep down inside we seem to realize this because, despite all our complaints about this world, we are like little babies at their mother's breast, needing to be weaned from our attachment to it (*Sermon 311,* 14).

Augustine believed that the appreciation of the beauty that surrounds us can lead to an awareness of God, its Creator. The beauty of the universe is so extraordinary that it simply cannot be explained as an accident. So, too, the amazing human power of "appreciating" that beauty must come from something more than their genetic codes. The only reasonable explanation for the beauty of the universe and the beauty of the human being is that both are reflections of the Infinite Beauty that is God (*Commentary on Psalm 26/2,* 12).

The beauty that we find in nature and in ourselves shows that God is here with us. God now works in the world by maintaining and governing all that he has made (*A Literal Commentary on Genesis,* 4.12.22), and he speaks to us through the glorious beauty of that world (*On Freedom of the Will,* 2.16.43). Looking at the beauty that surrounds us, we begin to understand Augustine's words: "The world smiles on us with many things, things of beauty, power, variety, but more beautiful is the one who made them" (*Sermon 158,* 7).

The Joy of Being Alive

In the Old Testament book of Psalms, the sacred writer gives a somewhat gloomy analysis of our life just now in this Hospice, this place of rest for travelers passing through:

> Our life is over like a sigh. Our span is seventy years or eighty for those who are strong. And most of these are emptiness and pain. They pass swiftly and we are gone. (*Psalm 90*, 10)

Perhaps the psalmist was having a bad day when he wrote such somber thoughts, but there is no denying the fact that most of us feel that way on at least some of our days. When that happens, when life goes sour and seems to be swiftly coming to an end, we may question the merits of this so-called "gift" of life itself.

Distress can come both in good times and bad times. If our life just now is good, we are distressed that it is coming to an end, that soon we must leave this pleasant place with its pleasant people forever. As Augustine said: "We want to live but are compelled to die. We want to live and try to lead a healthy life of good food and frequent exercise but dying is forced upon us anyway" (*Sermon 229H*, 2).

Our distress with life is even worse when our life is bad. If we are enslaved in an unhealthy life devoid of meaning and love, we may come to wonder why living was imposed on us in the first place. Hopefully we will experience some joy in life before we come to die, but some seem to be denied even such momentary pleasures in their lifetime. Human history testifies that

1. Many humans live hungry and die hungry after a short (or worse, long) painful life.
2. Many humans live anonymous lives as the refuse of society, living lives that are not worth much to others or even to themselves.
3. Many live and die alone, without knowing for any length of time the experience of love.
4. Finally, many live, if not as slaves of some human master, then as slaves to their own addictions, their own sickness, their own disability, the prison of limited opportunity.

Times have not changed that much. Augustine gave a vivid description of the troubles of living in fifth-century Africa:

> We all experience how distressing, how full of complaints this life is. We are beset by trials and temptations, full of fears, feverish with all kinds of greed, subject to accidents. We grieve when things go badly and are smugly self-satisfied when they go well. We are elated when we make a profit and in agony when we suffer losses. Even as we rejoice over our winnings, we begin to dread losing what we have gained. We fear being investigated now that we are a success (a threat we never had to face when we were failures). Those at the bottom of the heap long to climb to the top; those at the top fear sliding down to the bottom. The "have-nots" envy the "haves"; the "haves" despise the "have-nots." Indeed, who can find the words to describe how thoroughly and obviously ugly this life is? (*Sermon 302, #2*)

And yet (he adds) "this ugliness has its lovers." As temporary and as troublesome as this life may be, most of us come to love it with an undying passion (*Sermon 335b, 3*). Both those who say they look forward to the oblivion of death and those who piously proclaim their desire for life beyond death still seem reluctant to give up their hold on this life too easily (*Sermon 280, 3*). Indeed, Augustine believed that such is our passion for this life that some would be satisfied if even the present imperfect life could last forever (*Sermon 229h, #3*). In the midst of their suffering, they complain that there are really only two things wrong with life in this Hospice:

1. Day in and day out it is *beastly!*
2. And, worst of all, it is *short!*

Despite the troubles and temporary nature of this life, Augustine never doubted that the gift of life is a great gift. Indeed, he believed that the human power to cocreate by giving life to another human being was the greatest proof that God had not given up on the fallen human race (*City of God*, 22.24). The gift of life to a human being makes possible a blessed life in eternity and even a pretty good life here in time.

When we are tempted to condemn God for the troubles of this world, we should remember that this dying life beset by so many troubles is not the life that God wanted for us. In the Old Testament book of Genesis, we read that the first humans were created in a paradise, which, though only meant as a temporary home, still did not have all of the troublesome aspects of the world in which we live just now. Unfortunately even in paradise humans had the power to fail, and this they did.

Could God have not done better? Why did he create those first humans in a place where they had the power to fail, a place where in fact they did fail? Why did he not bring us into life with full vision of his goodness so that it would be impossible for us to make bad decisions? Why did he not create us in the stability of eternity rather than in transient time?

The only reasonable explanation is that he did not do so because he wanted to give us the challenge of discovering him in the midst of our passing days, days that are sometimes good and sometimes bad. If he had created us in heaven with the beatifying vision of his face, we would not have had the opportunity to search for him, to "want" him, to "want to believe," to "want" to see him. We would not have had the challenge to "choose" the still hidden God in the midst of the more evident and seemingly more delightful earthly goods. Put simply, if we had been created in the great, wonderful "outdoors" beyond this Hospice, we would never have been challenged to do the things that needed to be done if we were to "check out" nobly at the end of our time here.

We have a thirst for life because we have been made in the image of the God who is life itself and he made us this way so that we might be driven to seek that eternal life that stretches beyond death. As Augustine told his friends, living a pleasant happy life here in the Hospice is sometimes not in our control, and our eventual dying and leaving this Hospice is never in our control, but to live forever happy thereafter IS in our control (*Sermon 229h, #3*). This fact alone should be enough to make life truly a joy.

The Joy of Loving

One of the great things about this Hospice, this temporary home we share with others who (like us) are waiting for their "check out" time, is that it is possible for any of us to love and be loved. This life is not always pleasant. When the dark times come, it is hard to make our way on our own. It is love that can enhance our good times and make our bad times bearable. If we are lucky, sometime in our life we will feel the passion felt by Augustine at sixteen, a romantic passion which he described in the simple words: "My delight was to love and be loved" (*Confessions*, 2.2).

Of course, this was not his first experience with love. As a baby he certainly must have loved his parents with the possessive love common in little kids, a love that cries when left alone, a love that always enjoys being picked up, a love that sometimes causes the little tyke to weld itself to its mother's leg lest it lose her. There is a type of affection here to be sure, but it is often an affection that rests on a desire for someone who can "protect" or a desire for someone who can "amuse." Augustine also probably had some sort of affection for the ruffians with whom he ran as an adolescent. They were friends, but it would be too much to say that they were "lovers." He liked their company but certainly had no interest in becoming "one with them" in body and soul.

The passion for romantic love that Augustine experienced at sixteen was quite different from his love for his parents and friends. His feeling for the young woman who was to become his "common-law wife" was not simply "love." It was *LOVE!*, a blinding, paralyzing desire to become "one" with her. Admittedly his feeling was highly physical, but his desire for intimate physical union was the beginning of a desire for some sort of spiritual union, a union of hearts, a union which kept the young lovers together for eleven years and produced a child, Adeodatus.

In its highest form, love is a wish that my "totality" should become one with the "totality" of my beloved. In loving another human this way, I want to become one with them body and soul. In loving God this way, I want all that I *am* to become one with all that he *is*. Both Augustine and Sacred Scripture give powerful expressions of how we feel when we are overcome with the ecstasy of loving and being loved. Augustine put it this way:

> The act of love, my friends . . . its power, its flowers, its fruit, its beauty, its allure, its nourishment, its drink, its food, its overpowering embrace . . . is everlasting. (*Commentary on the Epistle of John,* 10.7.3)

Similar sentiments are expressed in God's love song to the human race, the Canticle of Canticles:

> For steadfast as death is love
> relentless as the nether world is devotion; its flames are a blazing fire.
> Deep waters cannot quench love,
> nor floods sweep it away.
> Were one to offer all he owns to
> purchase love, he would be roundly mocked. (Canticle 8:6-7)

Finding love in this Hospice as we wait to leave, having affection for others, having true and deep friendships with some human beings and romantic relationships with a few, can make this fleeting life bearable and even enjoyable, so enjoyable indeed that sometimes we don't want to leave even though we know that this is not our permanent home.

Such reluctance to leave may not be present if we are all alone. In my various motel experiences I was never tempted to stay more than absolutely necessary when I was by myself. I found myself longing for the great "outdoors" where dwelt all those whom I loved and who loved me. Most of the staff in the inn were pleasant enough but I can't say that they especially *loved* me. I was "room 328" rather than "Donald." I could get fine "room service" but I never found "love" on the menu.

Being with someone you love makes time in this Inn for Travelers enjoyable. During the day you have shared experiences, and in the evening you are never alone. Of course, even in the company of a lover, most sensible people are not tempted to extend their stay forever. This is not because they are not having a good time in the arms of their lover but because they are still not "home." They look forward to the day when the trip is over and they are able to return home with the one they love. Unfortunately in this life it is not always possible to leave at the same time. Most lovers exit life at different times, and even when we die together my death is always a solitary event. Other may witness my leaving, but they cannot share it.

We are creatures who are "in love with loving," and there is little we can do to avoid the pain that sometimes comes with love. Sometimes we love each other in a wrong way, over-emphasizing the physical pleasure that comes from it. Some desire only sexual release without any wish to become "friends" with their partner, to be "one in heart" with them. Infected with such perverse love, our desire for the "other" involves no "care for" or "care about" them. Indeed, our apparent passion for the "other" is really only a "passion" for self-satisfaction.

Such physical passion is far different from the love that God meant us to have for each other (and for him) when he made us "creatures who could love." Such purely carnal "loving" obviously does not make us better human beings. Indeed it makes us less decent than our animal friends. At least their season of "rutting" is restricted to certain times of the year and has as its goal the continuation of the species. For the carnal human the season of "rutting" is anytime there is a willing partner, and if offspring result they are viewed as "unfortunate" accidents.

When our romantic desire for others is merely physical (as it was in the beginning for Augustine), it creates a fragile bond easily broken. Although Augustine did stay faithful to his common-law wife for sixteen years, he was not above sending her away when she stood in the way of his career. Only after his conversion was he able to live up to the ideal of love, a union of hearts in which two become one in friendship.

Even when our love is pure, it can cause us pain. The desire to have another for a lover may not be reciprocated by the other person and we may be forced to carry such unrequited love in our hearts to our grave. And even when the love is mutual and intense, there still can be problems. Because of the circumstances of their lives, the lovers may not be able to consummate their love through an intimate union of body and spirit. And even when they can, there is always the likelihood that they will eventually be separated by death.

In the midst of the pain of losing our beloved, we may begin to wonder whether it is indeed better "to have loved and lost than never to have loved at all." In the depths of our distress we may call out to God: "WHY? Why did you make me a creature susceptible to such love, knowing that someday my love would cause me so much pain?" The fundamental answer to such a deeply felt question is that God created me a "loving" creature because he wanted to create a creature as close as possible to himself. Just as God is an infinitely and eternally *living* being, so, too, is God an infinitely and eternally *loving* being. He wanted to bring into existence a creature who would be capable of love just as he is a God of infinite love.

Furthermore, it was God's intention that we would someday be eternally united with him in heaven. We are certainly not there now; we are still on earth. We are not yet living in eternity; we are still living in time. For us to eventually achieve union with God, we must move from where we are to where we are meant to be. It is only through love that we can be moved from here to there. Created with a thirst for infinite happiness and eternal love, we are drawn into the future that God wants for us. Without desire, without love, there would be no movement. We would be no better than rocks held in place by blind forces beyond our control.

We are blessed if we have given our love to another human being because this prepares us to give ourselves in love to the Lord when he comes. Having given ourselves to another in love, having forgotten about ourselves for the sake of our human love, we open up space in ourselves for God. Our love stretches us. We reach out of ourselves to a good that is beyond ourselves. We become bigger as our spirit strains towards the good that is our beloved. Just as our heart and mind and spirit (nurtured by memory of time together that once was) can continue to live in the place of a lover now far distant, so, too, we can learn to live in a land of love that is our future, a land where we will walk forever in the embrace of our Lord.

Our deep love for other human beings who are distant from us can give us practice in loving the still unseen God. Can I truly love someone who is far away? Yes, indeed! I do so every day. Some of my loves live in distant places. Some of my loves have traveled across the chasm of death. I no longer can see many of my distant loves, but I am warmed by their memory. I am comforted by my dreams of them. I look forward to being with them again someday. I know that I have not lost my absent loves because the ache of their absence throbs in my every "here" and my every "now."

The skeptics cry: "Seeing is believing!" But no one can claim that "seeing causes loving" nor that "loving depends on seeing." We do not love everyone we see, nor do we need to constantly "see" someone in order to "love" them. Love is not seeing. Love is *choosing,* and I can choose and be chosen even though separated by space and time from my beloved.

We are blessed if we can wait for the Lord in the embrace of another human being who loves us. No human love can take the place of divine love but true human love can help us wait for the Lord in hope. Having experienced the love of another human being, of being loved despite our quirks and scars, can make it easier to believe that we can be loved by a God.

Indeed, the glory of human love is that our love for each other makes God present to us and in us even in the midst of our days in this Hospice. St. John told his friends that God is with us when we are truly joined to another human being in love. And who knows? Perhaps our passion for each other is God's way of holding us in his arms. Of course, Jesus could do the job himself but the line would be immense. He could not be available to us every time we needed him. And thus he often holds us during these days through the arms of a human love. Through them God is able to look on our wounds and our weakness and say, "I love you anyway" and then hug us very, very tightly. We don't know what the Lord will look like when he comes to us at the end of time, but this we know for certain: however he comes, he will come as a lover. Indeed, he comes to us now through the passion of our human loves. In their depth of feeling for us we can get some hint of the passionate love of God for each one of us.

When we leave our loves behind as we exit this life, their love will make it easier to go. We will be indeed sorry to leave them behind (and our passion for them may make us fight death as long as we can) but our experience of their love will give us some hope and even confidence that we will find love again in that great unknown world outside the doors of this Inn.

It is in that world beyond the doors that we will for the first time clearly hear God singing his great love for the human race, the song that echoes even now in the hearts of human beings who are truly in love:

Arise, my beloved, my beautiful one,
and come!

See, the winter is past
  the rains are over and gone.
The flowers appear on the earth,
  the time of pruning the vines has come, and the song of the
  dove is heard in the land.
Arise, my beloved, my beautiful one,
  and come! (Canticle 2:10-13)

A Solitary Life

In my travels through the various hotels and motels of this earth, I have often felt very much alone. This was especially true when I was sitting among strangers at a less than interesting academic conference. At the end of the day I would find myself in my room with a deep-felt need to talk to someone I loved, someone who seemed to care about me. This led to long phone calls, difficult to explain on my expense account. In my experience, bursars in charge of college expenditures have little appreciation for the need to have loving conversations from time to time.

Over the years I have come to understand that my solitary experiences in the hotels of the land were not unusual. As we live out our days in the Hospice that is this world, many of our hours will be solitary. We ride to work each morning in the crowded train or trolley or bus, each of us wrapped tightly in our own cell of solitariness. Even the well-to-do, who speed down restricted commuter lanes to their offices in their shining cars, are sometimes caught traveling with blown-up dummies in lieu of the required companions. The homeless in our cities often live lives of isolation with nowhere to go and no one to care. The elderly who have outlived their friends and family sometimes must spend their last days alone, being ministered to by strangers.

What makes such solitariness so difficult to bear is that we are social animals. We need some interaction with those who love us in order lead happy lives. Being with strangers at conferences, passing them on the street, lining up behind them at the super-market check-out counter is not enough. In those situations we are anonymous, "a person who was not really there." The crowds seem to be looking through us and beyond us searching for something more interesting.

Certainly there is no escape from living a solitary life deep inside our "self." As Augustine observed: "within our consciousness there is a great solitude which no one but ourselves can see and enter in" (*Sermon 47*, 23). Oh, it is true that we can try to tell others what we think, what we really mean by our words, what the context is that explains why we think the way we do, but such mysteries can seldom be revealed to others, even when we understand them ourselves. Augustine gives the reason:

> As we make our pilgrim way through life, each of us is encased
> in flesh and through that fleshy armor the heart cannot be seen.
> As long as we live in these bodies of ours each one carries their
> solitary heart and every heart is closed to every other heart.
> (*Commentary on Psalm 55*, 9)

Even physically most of us spend many hours of the day by ourselves. When I was teaching philosophy, I realized one day that despite the number of people I dealt with on any given day, at least half of that day was spent by myself. Of course, I had to be alone when I was preparing classes or marking exams, but even when I was proclaiming the truths of metaphysics to the uncomprehending crowd, I sometimes found myself thinking about something entirely different. Through my voice I was in contact with the class, but in my thoughts I was in another world and that world was solitary.

Teaching in a classroom presupposes the presence of others, but serious thinking about what to teach cannot be done in the midst of gabbling hordes. This is the reason why the insomniac Augustine did most of his writing at night. Most likely it was in the midst of such quiet moments, as he thought about the business and "busyness" of the next morning, that he was moved to cry:

> If only our minds could be seized and held still! Then we might be able to see the past, present, and future from the perspective of that eternity which governs all of the times of this life. (*Confessions*, 11.11)

For Augustine, contemplating at night in his quiet room, solitariness was a voluntary choice, but sometimes physical and spiritual isolation is forced upon us by circumstances beyond our control. Even if we could avoid facing such solitariness in life, we must face it at death. For every human being death is a solitary event. It is like the life we have in the womb before birth. The only difference is that birth is an unconscious event, neither anticipated nor remembered, while death is for most of us consciously anticipated and experienced.

Being a solitary in life and death is, then, a fact but there is no reason to fear it. Indeed, it may be the only circumstance where we can find true peace. Augustine tried to explain this in a letter to a friend:

> God speaking in the Scriptures promises: "I will make a covenant of peace with my sheep so that they may live tranquilly in the desert and sleep serenely in the quiet forests" (Ezekiel 34:25). By the phrase "in the desert" God means "in the solitude of each person's conscience." There we can rest quietly with our attention withdrawn from all the noise of the world outside. In that inner solitude we can rest by the streams of memory, remembering the words God spoke to us in the Scriptures. (*Sermon 47*, #23)

In the midst of our quiet solitude, we can rest and watch the rest of the world go by. In such moments of contemplation, we are not running away from the world; we are putting it in its proper place. Certainly our desire for solitude can never justify ignoring others. Charity demands that we try to reach out beyond our solitariness to help those in need (*Letter 48*, 2-3). Both action and contemplation are needed in our lives (*City of God*, 19.19), but the story of Martha and Mary in the New Testament and the story of Creation where God sanctified his day of rest rather than his days of activity show that restful solitude is more important than a life consumed by frenzied involvement in the world outside (*A Literal Commentary on Genesis*, 4.14.27).

Solitariness, when rightfully used, can be an instrument for happiness both in this life and in the next. In the depths of our solitary self we can speak again to loved ones who are no longer with us and speak to that God who is always with us but hiding deep within. It took many years for Augustine to develop such solitariness, but when he achieved it he cried out in joy:

> Late have I loved you, O Beauty ever ancient and ever new! Late have I loved you! Just think about it! You were there inside me when all the while I was searching for you outside myself. I was looking for you outside and I threw myself upon all those beautiful things that you had made. You were here with me, but I was off someplace else looking for you. (*Confessions*, 10.27.38)

Postscript: Reflection on an Empty Swing

There is a nice swing outside my window, a two-person swing just fine for swaying back and forth with someone you love. I sat in it the other day but I was by myself. It was somewhat pleasant sitting there. There was a light breeze cooling my "fevered" brow. (In a fit of exuberance I had just walked more than a mile.) The trees were just beginning to explode in their springtime green and, as though anticipating the good days coming, the birds chirped merrily as they flew from budding limb to budding limb. In the distance I could hear the sounds of children's games and the excited laughter of young lovers walking hand in hand in the growing twilight. I swung gently on my two-person swing and thought how wonderful it would be to have beside me the ones I loved. But they were at a distance and my only companion was my own solitariness.

Still, I was not especially lonely because I was filled with memories of good times past. I thought to myself that "remembering" is sometimes better than "seeing." Good times past can only be remembered; they cannot be recaptured. In my own case, I am no longer the vivacious (or so I thought) youth I once was, and those I walked with then have certainly changed too. Meeting again in present times might come as a shock to all of us. But the past pleasant times of laughter and shared affection are forever unchanged in memory. Perhaps that is the great delight in being able to swing alone in my two-person swing. In my imagination I can make present those I walked with in the past, remembering them as they were then and forgetting for a moment that those wonderful times are unlikely to ever come again.

One Paw Short of Perfection

The glory and the pain of being a human being is that we are driven to ask questions like the following:

What is it to be a human being?
Who am I?
Where am I now and where am I going?

Asking such questions is a sign of our glory because it is a sign that we are "thinking" beings. We have the power to try to figure things out, important things like life and death, joy and sorrow, love and hatred, health and sickness. We have the power to try to understand the universe in which we live and, more importantly, the universe that is our "self."

But this power of reflection is also a source of pain because trying to understand our "self" and the world is always difficult and sometimes the answers that we discover are not the answers that we wish to hear, for example, learning the humbling truth: "You do not have an inferiority complex; you really *ARE* inferior. Indeed, you have never been as good as you pretend to be." Considering all the disturbing things we can find out about ourselves, we can understand why the Spanish philosopher Unamuno wrote that "consciousness often seems to be a disease."

We discover important truths about life in many different ways, sometimes through a conversation or a lecture or a book.

Insight into the nature of my life came from watching a dog named Buck. Buck is a black male of middle age (neither a puppy nor an "old goat") and indistinguishable ancestry who frequently and excitedly runs through the Villanova campus under the supposed direction of a lagging master and mistress.

His human masters followed a straight and narrow path but Buck roamed far and wide, running vigorously to investigate anything new and interesting that he might come across, a nut-bearing squirrel, a passing rabbit who has stayed too long in the open meadow, a new flower of interesting smell, and, of course, any passing human who showed the least sign of being friendly. Buck's masters seemed pleased with his roaming. They smiled as he rushed here and there, perhaps wishing that they could join him in his romp. But they could not. They seemed trapped by accustomed paths, paths formed and cemented through open spaces as if to say to them: "This is the way you must go and no other! This is your place! To wander off the secure concrete way laid out for you is to invite disaster! Step lively because you have only so much time to accomplish your appointed task—to strengthen your debilitating body so that you can do exactly the same thing tomorrow and tomorrow and tomorrow."

Buck heard no such restrictive messages. He roamed far and wide as the wonder of life drove him. He did not "stay in any one place." Every place was his place and he testified to this fact by leaving his mark on whatever tree or rock was handy. His masters walked sedately down their fixed black-topped path, every once in a while calling Buck back from his joyful running through the universe that God had given him. What made all this interesting to me as I sat in my chair viewing the world outside (in a sense more immobilized than Buck's master and mistress) was that Buck accomplished all of his joyful running *with only three legs.* Like his masters and like you and me, old Buck was "One paw short of perfection." Unlike his masters (and you and me) Buck had no trouble accepting his disability and being joyful none the less. He ran through life on three legs but with a smile on his face.

Though his lack of a paw did not seem to bother him, I must believe that there were times when it was at least an inconvenience. The paw that was missing was in the front and although he was able to hop around quite merrily, he certainly could not sit up and beg as nicely as his more powerful and "pawfull" confreres. He had only one paw to wave and attract attention, but his one-paw prayer seemed unusually effective, even more effective than the prayer of those who had more paws. Buck's prayer was always humble; with only one paw to wag in the air, it would have been silly for him to put on airs.

Buck was disabled but was happy nonetheless and he did seem to have a full life. His masters seemed to love him, accepting him for what he was. Even his own kind seemed to like him. One night Buck was joined in his running by another dog of similar breed but with a full complement of legs. They ran together here and there with no one getting the upper paw. His friend (likewise a male) accepted him as a true brother. If he recognized his friend's deficiency, he did not make a big thing out of it and certainly did not seem to use it to his advantage. Buck was gifted with one of the great blessings of life: a true friend who tolerated his deficiencies, one whose disabilities (and all us old dogs have our own peculiar sort) offset his. Their relationship demonstrated the comforting fact that when you have a friend who, like you, may be "one paw short of perfection," you can stand straight and strong together by leaning on one another, supporting the other's weakness with your strength.

Certainly neither pooch seemed disabled as lovers. One night I saw them race towards a fair maiden of a different breed. Buck seemed as acceptable to the lady as his more pawed friend. She seemed to acknowledge the fact that any old dog is worthy of love even with certain disabilities, that love even with a dog "one paw short of perfection" could stand on its own two feet once one got beyond exteriors, once one was able to see both the good and the bad in the lover. Buck was just as acceptable to the young maiden as his more pawed friend. Though disabled, Buck was able to stand tall on his own (three) feet.

All things considered, Buck's world was a joyful world. He had a good friend with whom he could romp; he had a master and mistress who promised a safe haven when his days of running were over; and now he had found a love who loved him with all of his deficiencies. No wonder that he lived out his sometimes difficult days with a smile on his face.

I believe that Augustine would have felt close to Buck because he knew that he, and every other human being, is much like that old dog. All of us go through life "one paw short of perfection." Of course, Augustine did not express the idea in that way, but his description is just as instructive. One day when a group of young Christians came to him and excitedly announced that they were going to establish a perfect community made up only of those who were perfect, Augustine broke out in laughter. He said to them: "How are you going to find such people? Don't you realize that we all have been put in a furnace and have come out of it a little bit *CRACKED?*" (*Commentary on Psalm 99, #8*).

What he was saying to them and all of us is that we are all cracked pots, one paw short of perfection, and we must face up to that fact every day. I may be destined for heaven, but just now I don't feel that good. I roll out of bed each morning in parts. I have knees that ache and a stomach that gets upset. Just now I sometimes have unreasonable fear of my future. Just now I sometimes have very justified remorse for my past. I am a professed religious, but that does not change things. Augustine once said that when you baptize a drunk all you get is a baptized drunk (*Sermon 151, #4-5*). So, too, when you profess a cracked pot, all you get is a professional cracked pot. I am a priest, too, but all that means is that I am an ordained cracked pot.

The conclusion is obvious. As long as we live, we will live in a cracked world. We must live with our own cracks and put up with the cracks in others. We must live with these cracks and move bravely on and not despair, and there *ARE* good reasons for hope. After all, we are still alive and there is an immense amount of good left in us. We are still able to love and have a chance to be loved in return. If we are lucky, we can be surrounded by friends despite our pomposity and "pawpaucity." If we are very lucky, we can find a love who overlooks our paucity of paw and sees what we have left as the "paws that refreshes."

And best of all, all of us share the gift of the happy Buck in having a master (God) and a mistress (the Blessed Virgin) who truly care for us. Moreover, we have the great gift of Jesus Christ, a Jesus who is not only our Lord-God but who is also our Doctor . . . a Doctor who comes not to condemn us for our defects, but who comes to heal them. It is no wonder that one day Augustine cried out to his people:

> The important thing is not to give up in the midst of the healing process. Remember that Jesus loved you when there was really nothing lovely about you at all. . . . Can you imagine what Jesus will do for you when you are cured, considering that he DIED for you when you were still sick and ungodly? (*Sermon 142*, #2 and 7)

Like the old "paw-deprived" dog Buck, we need to be joyful in the midst of our disabilities. We need to sing. And not the sad words of the somber *DIES IRAE* that we used to sing at funerals. Rather we should sing a song like the hymn Augustine once wrote to the only Doctor he ever trusted completely, Jesus the Lord. It is the song of Buck to the master and mistress who cared about him. It is the song of cracked humans who finally realize that they are loved by an infinite God who dwells with them and in them as they go through life. Thinking about such wonderful things, Augustine sang:

> O Wonderful Healer, you care for us all:
> Soothing our painful swelling,
> Supporting our fading strength,

Cutting away the useless in our lives,
Keeping only the truly necessary,
Saving those given up for lost,
Giving beauty to those warped and bent by life.
Who can despair of life
Seeing how the Son of God has come down to help us?
(*The Christian Combat*, 11, 12)

Fever

As we live through our days in this Hospice, sometimes our spirit is overcome by a blazing fever. Of course, our old body will also get overheated from time to time, but such physical fevers seem somehow less distressing. There is always an aspirin to take or a potion to drink or a kind friend (usually not of the medical profession) who will advise their own folk medicine to help us in our time of need. The fevers of our spirit are not so easily cured. Indeed, we are often too embarrassed to admit that we have them. These fevers are passions like fiery lust, blazing anger, deep dark hatred, consuming envy, a hunger for revenge, the insatiable craving for money or power.

Because we are combinations of body and spirit, a fever in one part of us affects the other. When the body is consumed by earthy passions (for food, for drink, for sexual satisfaction), it is hard for the spirit to think of anything else. When the spirit is consumed by the fevers of anger or hatred or revenge or a passion for money or power or worldly success, our blood-pressure rises, our stomach gets upset, and we turn again and again on our beds through nights of sleepless anxiety. Some mathematicians have been known to cry "Eureka!" when solving a particularly abstruse problem. Some artists have glowed with ecstasy at seeing their finished work. Even some philosophers have danced for joy when they thought they had discovered the mystery of "being."

There should be no surprise at such physical manifestations of joy and sorrow. Our emotional life is as much a part of our human nature as is the life of the mind. God did not make us to be unfeeling intellects; he made us warm bodily creatures who could think. As Augustine observed, no one with any sense would condemn a person for being angry with evil people in order to correct them, or for being sad for suffering people in order to help them feel better, or for fearing lest a loved one die. Our emotional reactions are good when the love that prompted them is good; they become evil only when the love is itself perverse (*City of God*, 14.6).

Augustine believed that apathy is not the Christian ideal; controlled fervor is. Indeed, he suggests that without some fervor in our lives, we can never hope to understand the divine passion for humans and the human passion to seek the infinite. It was probably because of this conviction that one day, when he was trying to describe to an unresponsive audience the joy of infinite love, he cried out: "Give me a person who is in love! They will know what I mean. But if I speak to a cold person, they will simply not know what I am talking about" (*Commentary on the Gospel of John*, 26.4).

Love is good in itself but a fevered love for anything besides God can become very destructive (*City of God*, 14.15). Augustine learned through experience that the fever of sexual obsession can dominate any human's life if not controlled. At such manic moments we want to *consume* the object of our infatuation, to possess them, to tie them down so that they cannot escape, to force them to become ours alone. Such passion is far from being true love. Indeed, we really do not care about the other person at all. What we want with all of our being is the satisfaction of the sexual desire that they have set ablaze in us.

Great age is no protection against such fevers arising. To make this point, Augustine told his friends the story of "an eighty-four year old man who, after living piously and chastely with his virtuous wife for twenty-five years, suddenly bought himself a female lyre player to satisfy his lust" (*Against Julian*, 3.11.22). The reasons for such strange behavior can be many.

Perhaps such passions in the old are fed by loneliness or boredom. At an age when it is sometimes hard to feel alive, a person may reach out for anything that promises to be exciting, especially when it brings back memories of a vigorous youth. Whatever the proximate reasons, such elderly escapades are just another sign that we remain human (and somewhat cracked) until the day we die.

Unfortunately, even if the fever of sexual passion begins to die with age, there is no assurance that some other fever will not take its place. Augustine observed that in his experience, when the passion for sex begins to diminish, very often avarice becomes more powerful (*On the Good of Widowhood*, 20.26). Certainly there is no age limit on the fever of anger, the fever of revengeful thinking, the fever of hatred, the fevered sadness of hurt feelings, the killing fever of despair. Though these fevers may not be as obviously flaming as the fever that comes with sexual obsession, they are fevers nonetheless. When one is infected, there is no energy or desire to do much good.

Augustine believed that the secret of "controlled and virtuous fever" is to train our various appetites as we might train young colts, using reins that are neither too slack nor too firm in order to channel their natural vigor towards the good (*Confessions*, 10.31.47; *On the Usefulness of Fasting*, 3.3). The part of us that needs the training is not so much our poor old body as our ever-young spirit. It is there that good and bad decisions are made. As in the equine analogy above, when trying to achieve a perfect union between horse and rider, it is not so much the horse that needs correction as it is the rider who either tends to let his steed drag him wherever it wishes or who destroys his faithful companion by unreasonable beatings and denial of true needs. In heaven after the resurrection, we shall be at peace with ourselves and with our horse (our bodies) (*Sermon 155*, 14.15), but just now there will always be need for cautious care of that sometimes rambunctious friend.

O Lord, Protect Me from Making a "Perverting Choice"!

> Our infancy demonstrates with what ignorance of the truth we enter life and our adolescence makes clear how full of folly and wild desires we are. In fact, if anyone were left to live as they pleased and to do what they desired, they would go through the whole gamut of lawlessness and lust, those sins which I have listed and perhaps many others that I forgot to mention. (*City of God*, 22.22.1)

—

William C. Tremmel, in an article published some time ago, wrote about a phenomenon called "A Converting Choice."[1] Through such a choice, the person suddenly makes a decision that makes their life forever different and better than what went before. As examples of such a choice, he cites the conversion of the confused and sometimes profligate Augustine, the change of the pharisee Saul from persecutor to proselytizer, the vision of Luther that prompted him to reject what went before and to begin to preach a different approach to Christianity. Tremmel also cites the more humble example of the drunk who, after years of worshipping the bottle, suddenly admits: "I am an alcoholic and I need help."

Looking at his own radical change of life for the better, Augustine saw it as a miracle of grace that God seemingly ignored all his wanderings and then flooded him with a grace that picked him up and enabled him to see and choose a life that was dedicated to Christ. Remembering his past experience, Augustine also realized that it was the same abundant grace that kept him faithful (though not sinless) for the next forty years and gave him the strength to persevere to the end.

Such stories are wonderful stories, stories that give us "cracked" humans hope that somehow or other we will get through life and be able to enter heaven. But there are other stories, stories that are not so pleasant, stories that can make us "shake in our boots" no matter how virtuous we pretend to be. These are stories of "perverting choices," decisions that inevitably change a human life for the worse.

My friend Bill told me such a story a few days before he died. He himself had led a somewhat mixed-up life but now, dying in the arms of God, he said: "You know, the most important thing in this confusing life is to never make a decision that becomes a perverting choice." The example he gave was that of a young basketball player who had recently graduated from college and had signed a contract to play for an NBA team at a salary that would forever rescue him and his family from their life-long poverty. In celebration of his good fortune, he went out to "party" with friends. With their encouragement he tried cocaine for the very first time. He died from its effects. For him that one choice to try drugs was indeed a perverting choice that not only made his life worse but ended it.

A similar sad case is what happened to a brilliant college professor. She was an accomplished teacher, loved by her students and respected by her peers. Soon after her marriage to a confrere she gave birth to a little girl. Sadly, the baby was born with a harsh form of Down's syndrome. Torn apart by postpartum depression exacerbated by seeing the suffering of her baby, the desperate mother killed her child. Although her depression argued for confinement and treatment in a mental facility, she was arrested and put in jail. A few weeks later she took her own life, unable to live with the memory of her terrible choice. There is great good hope that she joined her baby in the arms of God, but the sad fact remains that she will probably be remembered here on earth more for the terrible things that happened at the end of her life than for her many accomplishments in earlier days.

If the classic example of a "converting choice" is the conversion of the apostle Paul, the classic example of a "perverting choice" must be the fall of the apostle Judas. Two days before the day on which Christ would be executed, Judas made the terrible choice to deliver Christ to his enemies (Matt 26:1-16). For the meager sum of thirty pieces of silver (in today's currency about $25.50), Judas agreed to betray his God. It was a decision that would forever defile his name. Ever after that perverting choice he would be remembered as "Judas the betrayer."

It is a shame that this should be so. There was certainly more to Judas' life than this one act. Perhaps if he had not made that decision to betray Jesus he would have been remembered as "Judas the good family man" (or) "Judas the devoted disciple" (or even) "Judas the skilled money-manager." Judas had spent *years* doing all these great good things. His one act of betrayal took only two days, but it is for this that he is remembered here on earth.

The real tragedy of Judas was that he became convinced that his terrible deed irreversibly changed the direction of his life for all eternity. Unlike Peter who had the hope-filled humility to make amends for his three-fold denial of Christ, Judas seemed to believe that his once only betrayal was irredeemable. Unable to forgive himself, he came to believe that he could not be forgiven even by Jesus-God. In a paradoxical mixture of despair and pride, he said to himself: "My sin is too great for even a God to forgive!" and he then went out and hung himself on a nearby tree.

The story of Judas warns us that a perverting choice is possible even in the best of circumstances. Judas had followed Jesus for many years. He had heard his preaching. He had seen the miracles. He had eaten with Jesus and joked with him. He had looked into the eyes of the Son of God, but even this immediate experience was not enough to overcome his greed, his ambition. Perhaps he thought that this Jesus would eventually come to rule the world and that he (Judas) would become his "right-hand man." Perhaps he believed that someday he would become rich by being a friend of the Lord of the Universe. He was not able to stand the fact of his Master's apparent failure, and thus when it was clear that Christ's enemies were becoming more powerful, he changed camps.

Certainly the list of possible perverting choices that we could make is endless, choices where one way or another we decide to throw over all that we had considered important to have an "experience" of the "other side," that delicious part of life that becomes delicious precisely because it is forbidden to us. The list is long because, in our present fragile existence with frail bodies and minds receptive to any passing fancy that promises pleasure, there seem to be thousands of ways in which we can ruin our own lives and the lives of those who care for us. Judas' decision to betray Jesus was a "just this once decision," not unlike the decisions we are tempted to make

- to drive while drunk "just this once," only to crash and kill an innocent family;
- to try this drug "just this once," only to have our search for "heaven" end in a "hell" of our own making;
- to have an affair "just this once," only to have the marriage to our one true love fall apart because of our discovered adultery;
- to cheat in a business deal "just this once," only to have our fraud uncovered and to be labeled untrustworthy for the rest of our lives.

The substance of such choices may be different but the effect on our lives is the same. We discover to our horror that our bad "just this once" decision has a "forever" effect. Our one perverting choice now comes to define our lives.

Some of these perverting choices are like time-bombs, detonating years after the decision was made. Some of my friends have suffered the loss of their careers for indiscretions long past that have now been revealed. Some of the couples I know have been forever stained by affairs years past that have suddenly surfaced, bringing sorrow to the innocent spouses and children who were affected by the long-ago "fling." In all such cases the perverting choice made in the past suddenly explodes and destroys the lives of those affected.

The grace of God required to prevent such sad perverting choices must be at least as powerful as the grace that supported "converting choices" in the great saints. Augustine received such amazing grace to make his own converting choice, but he also admitted that the same level of grace had been required during his bad days to prevent them from becoming even worse. Looking back on his mixed-up youth, he did not dare to claim: "Well at least I had the moral strength to avoid adultery." He knew that he could not take credit for that omission because he heard God saying:

> Even in the depths of your worst days I was preserving you for myself. Sometimes the reason why you did not commit adultery was because there was no one to tempt you. There was no one to tempt you because *I* made sure there was no one there to tempt you. At other times the time and place of adultery were not available. It was *I* who made sure they were not available. The reason why you did not consent even when there was someone there to tempt you and the time and place were available was because *I* frightened you off. Just as you are in my debt for the grace *forgiving* you for the evil you have done, you are also in debt to me for the grace that *prevented* you from doing even worse. (*Sermon 99*, 6)

It is a great grace that gives the strength to "pick up the pieces" and get on with life after a perverting choice has had its destructive effect. In this regard, I have known couples who in some way or other have been able to get beyond the failures of the past and live somewhat happy lives. I suspect that often there was a "cloud" darkening the relationship, but by the grace of God it was possible for them to see the light of love that still remained.

Grace to cope with a changed life is certainly needed by those who have lost careers as a result of their past perverting choice. I think here of those who ministered to others but who are now forbidden to practice that ministry because of the past evil they had done. I think here not only of those whose evil actions really happened, but also of those where the evil was the fabrication of an accuser. Unfortunately the accusation alone is sufficient in many cases to prevent the accused from continuing their career in the ministry.

Perhaps for a while the terrible effects of a perverting choice will not be made public. Perhaps after your drunken accident you will be able to escape home with no one the wiser. Perhaps your "one time only" sexual escapade can be hidden from the true love of your life. Perhaps your cheating will not be discovered. But even when this happens, you are still left with the burden of memory. Such a memory may prevent you from becoming a fool again but also it may cause a fear that after so many years your failure will become public and the world you have constructed so carefully for yourself will fall apart.

All of us, saint or sinner, are well advised to pray to be protected from making any perverting choice. If it is too late for such prayers, then we should pray for God's forgiveness and the forgiveness of those whom our stupid perverting choice has injured. We know God will forgive even the worst offense (even Judas may have been saved), but it is not as certain that those who live around us in this life will ever be able to forgive or forget what we have done. And perhaps worst of all: we may never be able to forgive ourselves.

1. William C. Tremmel, "The Converting Choice," *Journal for the Scientific Study of Religion* (Spring, 1971) 17ff.

Forgiveness

When you are told "Your enemy is asking your pardon," you
must forgive straightaway. If you don't forgive your enemy then,
you are not only deleting the Lord's Prayer from your heart,
you are deleting yourself from God's book. (*Sermon 56*, 16)

The old movie "Love Story" contained the charming but
inaccurate principle: To be in love means to never need to say
"I'm sorry." It is inaccurate because living in this world of
"cracked people" we must *always* be prepared to say "I'm sorry."
This world is not made livable because we are perfect, because
we never hurt those we love, because we never rage against
strangers for real or imagined injuries. It is only made livable
because we sometimes have the courage to make amends for
the injuries we have done to others and to forgive the injuries
done to us.

It is not surprising that as long as we live in this Hospice,
this Inn for Travelers, there will be need for forgiveness. Augustine once remarked that all humans have enemies (*Sermon
56*, 14). The reason for this is that, although we are all going in
the same direction, we have different agendas and different
conditions of body and spirit. The only things that all of us
share are our desire for life and love and meaning and freedom

and the fact that all of us are "cracked." As a result, the ways in which we choose to fulfill our desires are often quite different and we come into conflict with others. Sometimes we decide that the only way we can achieve happiness is by taking care of ourselves, and in pursuit of that goal we become indifferent to the injury that our actions cause to others.

A sad fact of life is that we don't need to go to the health club to acquire bruises in this Inn. We can run against each other in any room in the facility. We can injure each other in an infinite number of ways even in that presumably "safe" room that we call home. This fact was brought to my mind the week after the 9/11 disasters in New York and Washington. I was hearing confessions at a neighboring retreat house and what struck me was that most of the folks I met did not speak of the upset they felt from the national disaster. What they agonized over and sometimes wept over were the little wars that were going on in their own private lives:

- children who rejected their parents and blamed them for their mixed-up lives;
- spouses who made unreasonable demands;
- friends who suddenly became cold and distant;
- a workplace poisoned by jealousy and conflict.

Unhappily, we need not go to foreign lands to find people who individually or collectively hate us and sometimes cause us injury. Indeed, it is more painful to be hated by someone who knows us and should love us than by some anonymous terrorist.

Forgiving others does not mean that we should not hold them accountable for the injuries they cause. Granted that this Hospice should be a place of loving goodness and loving forgiveness, it also must be a place of loving justice, and this means that actions that injure others should be condemned. If injustice is not offset by justice, the impression can be created that an act of hatred is no different from an act of love. Reason itself cries out against such fallacy. As Augustine says:

For us to be truly virtuous, we must not only do no harm to any person but we must also restrain them from wrongdoing and punish the evil that they in fact do. We must do this in order that the person punished may profit from the experience of being punished or at least that others will be warned not to do the same thing themselves. (*City of God*, 19.16)

As individuals we must condemn the evil that others do, but we have no right to punish them if we have no authority over them. A parent may punish the wrongdoing of their young children in order to train them in doing the right thing. The community may punish those who break its rules, but we as individuals have no right to return injury for injury by "getting back" at those who injure us. The only recourse we have is to try to forgive them, even though we can perhaps never forget what they have done to us. This is necessary not only because of our Christian principles but also to avoid injuring ourselves. Augustine noted long ago that anger nourished turns to hatred and hatred destroys us. Only forgiveness can put the hurt behind us and begin our recovery. As he urged his listeners: "Let's not bear grudges. The more we bear grudges, the more they rot our hearts" (*Sermon 114*, 4).

Even the worst of humans is still a reflection of God. In all of us it is a tarnished image, and in the very wicked it may seem to be an image that has been obliterated. But it is still there and there is always the possibility of a change of heart in even the worst of us. As long as our persecutors exist, we must resist the temptation to angrily destroy them. Rather, we must try to give them the opportunity for such change of heart.

Augustine believed that there is little we can do to eliminate anger from our lives as long as we live in this Inn for Travelers (*Sermon 211*, 1). Our "cracked" personality and our infinite thirst for "good" establishes the condition for a "life-rage" against any and all who seem to be getting in our way. In this imperfect life we can never get all the good things that we desire. In this imperfect life, there will often be a just cause for anger when we see

the evil inflicted on the innocent, when we see the evil and stupid things we and others sometimes do. At times anger will "well
up" even against those we love most dearly. All we can do is try
not to express it, try not to nourish it. People talk about becoming a "prisoner of love," but we can also become enchained by
anger even against those we love and this anger can lead to a hatred (*Commentary on Psalm 30*, 4). Such hatred then becomes our
prison. As Augustine cautioned his listeners:

> People who hate others walk about and come and go as they
> please. They are bound by no chains. But I don't want you to
> think that those who are angry are not imprisoned. Their prison
> is their heart. (*Sermon 211*, 2)

Such hatred makes it impossible to love either God or other
humans. Hatred is a darkness that completely eliminates the
illumination that true love brings into our lives (*Commentary
on Psalm 54*, 8). Even if our hatred is never expressed in action
and thus hurts no one else, it gradually destroys us (*Confessions*, 1.18.28). We become an enemy to ourselves (*Sermon 82*,
3), gradually closing off our lives until no human, no God, can
enter in (*Commentary on Psalm 134*, 1). We turn back upon ourselves, hugging our angry hatred more and more tightly until
our spirit dies of strangulation. As Augustine warned:

> Love is our life. If love is life, then hatred is death. Someone in
> a fit of rage may kill another's body but when you hold onto
> hatred, you kill your own soul. The murderer kills a body; you
> kill your spirit. (*Commentary on Psalm 54*, 7)

The only force that can stop the development of such hatred is forgiveness. It is only by a forgiving love of others that
we can overcome the viciousness that sometimes seems to dominate our times (*Commentary on Psalm 54*, 5). All of us are in a
place for healing, a Hospice, where bruised pilgrims rest and
recuperate for the road ahead. We must accept that each one of
us is wounded and give each other the opportunity and the time

to heal. Unquestionably, it is hard to forgive when someone is nailing our body and spirit to a cross. Clearly we must condemn what they have done, but on some occasions, at least, we need to repeat the words of Christ on his Cross: "Forgive them Father, for they know not what they do" (Luke 23:34).

The Search for Peace

Commenting on the fifteenth verse of Psalm 33 [34] "Seek peace and pursue it," Augustine told his listeners:

> Scripture does not promise us that we will have peace here but still we should seek it and pursue it. The psalm urges us to "seek peace and pursue it," because when we have risen from the dead, our corruptible part will be transformed and we will then finally be able to be at peace. In heaven there will be no one to trouble us any more. (*Commentary on Psalm 33/2*, #19)

It is a somewhat depressing comment. We are urged to seek peace and then are told that we will never achieve it in this life. It is like telling a little kid about the wonders of Disneyland and adding, "But of course you cannot go there just now."

If there is one thing we seek in life, it is peace. As Augustine says, there is nothing that we talk about so frequently, so fervently desire, so welcome when possessed, in a word, so good for us as peace (*City of God*, 19.10). We all thirst for peace, hunger for peace, and this is the reason why it is hard to achieve. Perfect peace means nothing less than "never being hungry" (*Commentary on Psalm 33/2*, #19), having all of our human hungers for life and meaning and love and freedom completely and permanently satisfied. In this life this will never happen. In this life we shall always be hungry.

Augustine does not deny that we can satisfy some of our hungers at least some of the time in this life, but our satisfaction is always limited by the fact that we are still living in an Inn for Travelers. Once a hunger is filled, it quickly returns when the "bread" or "important job" or "love of our life" or "health-filled days" depart. As he says:

> It is true that here on earth you can sometimes find bread to ease your hunger but once the bread is gone the feeling of warfare raging in your empty stomach returns. (*Commentary on Psalm 33/2, #19*)

Even if we do sometimes satisfy our hungers here on earth, our delight in fullness can only be fleeting. Our life and all the things we enjoy in life are only part of our transient existence in this Hospice. We must someday move on. We are here for rest, not residence (*Commentary on Psalm 34/1, 6*). If we enjoy good health at the present moment, it inevitably diminishes. If we have importance, it inevitably wanes. If we have found love, there is no guarantee that our beloved will be with us forever. If today we have freedom to do and go where we wish, tomorrow bad health can rob us of our mobility. Our freedom today to be creative in our work can tomorrow be taken away by a new boss who does not understand or appreciate what we are trying to do. Fame lasts only for a fleeting moment, and when we die it ceases to be of any importance at all. Love is a precious gift, but we may fall out of love or have our loves fall out of love with us. It is no wonder that Augustine will hold out little hope (indeed, *no* hope) for *perfect* peace in this life.

There are at least three reasons for this. *First*, there are just not enough goods in this life to satisfy our hunger for the infinite. Even if we had everything anyone could wish for in this life (Augustine lists such things as money, a large family, blameless sons, pretty daughters, full cupboards, plenty of cattle, no ruined walls or broken fences, no tumult or quarreling in the streets, nothing but quiet and peace, an abundance of wealth in the home and in the state), the best that can come from possessing all these great good things is a temporary and incomplete sort of peace. It does not fulfill all our desires because it is impermanent, tied to material things and therefore destined someday to perish (*Commentary on Psalm 143*, 18).

The *second* reason why it is so hard to find peace in this life is that we seem to be constantly in a state of conflict. For our peace to be perfect there must be the permanent absence of strife and dissension. But where in this world can you find such harmony? It seems to demand a world that is truly "One" and we live in a universe of the "Many." In the really existing world of multiplicity, peace can only be found in an *ordered tranquility*, an arrangement of like and unlike things whereby each of them has its own proper place (*City of God*, 19.13.1). Unfortunately, as long as there is life this side of death, there will be *conflict*, parts striving for better places, impinging on the places of others, neglecting the place where they are meant to stay. Each day we face the internal conflict of a body slowly falling apart and a soul dreaming of being more than it can be. Externally we fight with others to get our fair share (and sometimes more than our fair share) of the limited goods available for our subsistence and pleasure.

This disharmony in life starts deep inside each one of us. We are often "at odds" with ourselves (*Commentary on Psalm 33/2*, 19). Sometimes we are torn apart by guilt about the past, by present conflicting urges, passions and addictions, by worry about achieving a future too perfect ever to be realized in this life. Internal peace can be accomplished only when all of our desires are well-ordered (*Commentary on Psalm 84*, 10). Perfect peace demands an internal and external harmony. Only when we are at peace with ourselves, can we begin to reach out in friendship to others, trying to bring about that oneness of heart (*concordia*) that is the basis for peace in the family, in the community, in the world at large (*City of God*, 19.13.1).

Creating peace within ourselves will always be a difficult task. As long as we live in our disintegrating body we must cope with our unruly flesh and weakened spirit. Only a person with no temptations, only a person who is finally free of hunger, thirst, illness, and tiredness can find a complete peace within themselves. Lacking that, there will always be a daily battle to be fought, an obstacle to be overcome (*Commentary on Psalm 84*, 10). In this life we are never free of anxiety. In the best of times the good things in life tempt us. In the worst of times we are in danger of despairing because of the evil we see all around us and deep within us (*Sermon 20a*, 1).

The *third* (and perhaps most important) reason why perfect peace is impossible in this life is that by its very nature it is impermanent. Everything we want and have during our stay in this Hospice must be left behind when our time comes to leave. As a result, our present satisfaction is frequently dulled by fear of losing what we have (*The Happy Life*, 2.11). For perfect peace to exist, it must be eternal (*The Morals of the Catholic Church*, 1.2.5).

This is not to say that we cannot find some peace in this life, but it must begin with an acceptance of the fact that we are indeed in a Hospice and that whatever happens to us in this life, it will pass. We must make our own the prayer of the psalmist:

> O Lord, make me realize the shortness of my life so that I may begin to achieve wisdom of heart. Let your blessing rest upon me and give success to the work of my hands. (*Psalm 90*, 12 and 17)

The "wisdom" that the psalmist speaks of is the acceptance that our times, our things, our friends are all passing. Like us, they are transient. Therefore the "success of the work of my hands" I must pray for is that I will be able to live through these passing times with enough integrity to achieve the perfect peace promised in eternity. Once I have developed that wise vision of life just now, I can begin to enjoy the true but passing peace that can be found in this life.

Finding some peace in this life is indeed possible. It will never be perfect but it will be no less real. In this life, as in the next, the foundation is love (*Commentary on Psalm 33/2*, 19). Thus, when we are sick and it seems that our desire for a healthy *life* is frustrated, there can be some peace from knowing others are sorry for our troubles. Even though we are failures in the eyes of a world that sees no *meaning* in our lives, we can still feel important if we are loved by someone. Our desire for *love* is indeed central to our lives, and luckily it can be nourished by even the least bit of affection expended and received. Though a fervent love that binds us tightly to another may seem to the outsider to threaten our desire for *freedom*, we know that it does not. Indeed, it fulfills the desire. No one is more free than those who are "imprisoned" in the arms of their beloved.

This does not mean that our hunger for love will be perfectly satisfied in this life. As Augustine remarks:

> It is impossible for disputes never to arise. Disputes break out even between saints like Barnabas and Paul (Acts 15:39). But these are not so destructive of the unity of hearts as to kill charity. (*Commentary on Psalm 33/2*, 19)

There will be disputes and even quarrels between the most fervent lovers, but if the love is strong it will endure, perhaps somewhat scarred but still firm. Of course, our love would be more perfect if such disputes never arose, but this is not likely to happen this side of death. We are too different and too much a mystery to each other for this to happen. It is for this reason that peace is more a gift of God's grace than a personal accomplishment (*City of God*, 15.4). Through that grace we can be strengthened in the midst of the pressures of life before death and can develop the confidence that our life after death will finally be free of all strife (*City of God*, 15.4).

Just now there is no escape from the imperfections that disturb our peace. As Augustine told his people: "The righteous themselves groan here below, brothers and sisters, in order to teach you that we may seek peace here but that we will obtain it only at the end of this life" (*Commentary on Psalm 33/2*, 19).

What he was telling them is that the turmoil that sometimes comes into our lives is not necessarily a punishment for our sins. It is just part of the human condition. Even the most advanced in virtue, those who are here and now at peace with themselves and the world, must carry on the battle to retain that peace (*Sermon 61a,* 7). Even for those who lead truly good lives in this life, their persistence in searching for perfect peace comes from a hope for what will come to them after death (*Commentary on Psalm 147,* 20).

Even though perfect peace in this life will never be achieved, we must continue to seek it here. If we have not fought for such peace in this life, we will not find it in the life to come. As Augustine warned his listeners:

> Seek peace, then brothers and sisters. In this life there is no true peace, no tranquility. We are promised the joy of immortality and fellowship with the angels. But anyone who has not sought it here will not find it on arriving there. (*Commentary on Psalm 33/2,* #19)

Dealing with Disaster

In 410 the Goths, a barbarian horde from the North, sacked the imperial city of Rome, which was then the center of western civilization. Two years later Augustine began his book *The City of God* in an attempt to explain why such disasters happen. Two passages seem especially relevant in these troubled times:

> We should all remember that the whole earth, like a stormy sea, is always beaten by the storm of such calamities. (*City of God*, 5.22)

And again:

> As unpredictable as humans are, no nation has ever been so secure as to be free from all fear of hostile attacks. (*City of God*, 17.22)

Perhaps one of the reasons why Augustine wrote such somber words was that he was beginning to enter old age. As we get older most of us begin to realize that all of the days of our flowing life will not be filled with sweetness and light. Sometimes disaster strikes and we are forced to face a new period in our lives, a time when we must confront the fact that our life and human life in general is a fragile and precious commodity.

I am not speaking here of the upsetting grief that comes from the loss of a loved one. Such loss is bad enough, but it does not usually make us believe that the world itself is falling apart. Nor am I speaking about the disruption that comes from natural disasters such as earthquakes and hurricanes, floods and fires. These disasters are only the earth telling us that it, too, is flowing into the future and warning us not to be destroyed by the motion.

The disasters I speak of here are the disasters inflicted on us by the violence of our own species, "cracked" humans like us who suddenly reach out and kill their own kind. This is not the violence of a tornado; it is the violence of a terrorist who kills thousands of innocents for the sake of some nebulous "cause." Such disasters are upsetting because many of us live with the assumption that humanity is a peaceful race, that all of us are good and sane and getting better. We never grow out of the optimism of our infancy, believing with a hopeful smile that any passing stranger will love us.

Unfortunately such unrestrained optimism is not supported by the evidence of history. Since the Fall from Eden, beginning with Cain's murder of his brother, every age has been tinged with violence. Humans die in wars. Criminals do deadly deeds that seem to cry out for fierce retribution. Terrorists use destruction to make a point. Others randomly kill the weak simply because they enjoy it.

Such disasters make us face the unpleasant reality that not all of our companions in this flowing life, that not all of those who live with us in this Inn for Travelers are very nice people. Indeed, on some days (hopefully few) even *we* are not nice people. We suddenly begin to realize that, given the right circumstances, any of us could lash out against our kin and cause early exits from this Inn. Sadly, in this truly beautiful Hospice, this place of rest for pilgrims, the fact is that we must sometimes deal with disasters caused by the ugliness of our own kind.

To deal with them we must first try to understand why they happen. As might be expected, various explanations have been offered by scholars over the years. Some have suggested that we humans are by nature aggressive animals, and the best we can do is to try to control this aggression by whips and lashes. They agree with the terrifying sentiments of Arthur Schopenhauer:

"Man is at bottom a savage, a horrible beast. We learn this quickly when we try to create civilization by taming and restraining him."[1] Others like Plato have suggested that we are often too dumb to be virtuous, that humans are violent because they lack education. Marx and Rousseau believed that bad action is the result of bad environment. Given the right environment, all of us would be saints.

My own view (shared by many others throughout history) is that most of us have the power to *freely choose* the direction of our lives. Even in a good environment we can choose to be "good and bad," and even in a bad environment we can (with the grace of God) choose to better ourselves. As Augustine wrote long ago: "All of us have within ourselves the means of doing what we are bidden" (*Commentary on Psalm 32/2*, 5). But, having said this, he adds that if we are free (and we are) it is at best a wounded freedom. We are good people who are "cracked," and it is this "crackedness" in human beings that explains why we are sometimes violent. Wounded will and darkened intellect are the culprits, not environment and not human nature.

No one is exempt from this flaw. All of us share a common disability and without the grace of God every one of us would falter. Perhaps because of his own wild and confused youth, Augustine was absolutely convinced that the tendency towards abject stupidity and uncontrolled passion is seeded in every one of us. Every one of us is born in ignorance and as soon as we become conscious all sorts of crazy desires begin to surface. As he remarks: "Our infancy proves with what ignorance of the truth we enter life and our adolescence makes clear to all the world how full we are of folly and wild desires" (*City of God*, 22.22.1).

Conscious of the woundedness he found in himself and in others, Augustine concluded that violence of human against human will always be part of human experience this side of death. This is so because the conflict at the root of violence is within each flawed individual. We are torn between the goods of this world and the promises of the next. At one and the same time we desire to be more than we can be while being tempted to be less than we are. We are dusty angels, looking to the heavens as we fight for the goods of this earth. We want everything and are jealous of those who have anything that is not ours. As a result

> Each individual in this community is driven by his passions to pursue his private purposes. Unfortunately, the objects of these purposes are such that no one person can ever be wholly satisfied. The effect is that this world remains in a chronic condition of civil war. There is the continuing oppression of those who fail by those who succeed. (*City of God*, 18.2.1)

This is not to suggest that we are all vicious animals all of the time. There are many truly good people in this world, and even the worst of us have some good moments. If Augustine were alive today and were asked, "What are human beings really like?" he would tell us that most of us, by the grace of God, are able to control the violent tendencies that sometimes well up in our hearts.

Strangely enough, it could be the great good that is part of our nature that sometimes makes us erupt violently against the restriction of our times. Those very natural desires that drive us into the future towards God can cause frustration. We are finite beings with a thirst for the infinite. We are imperfect beings who desperately want everything to be perfect. We are beings with a thirst for life, meaning, love, and freedom but none of these desires can be perfectly or permanently satisfied as we go through this flowing life. When any of these great goods are threatened, we may reach out and try to bring down with us anyone who seems to stand in our way.

As long as we live in this "cracked" world, the truth spoken by Augustine in the late fourth century will continue to be true: "Our peace depends on the sworn oaths of barbarians not only at home but throughout the world" (*Letter 47*, 2). As individuals we cannot change the course of world events. All that we can control in our days of disaster is the nobility of our own lives and the love and respect we give to those around us. Perhaps we cannot do much for those destroyed or injured by the hatred of other human beings. But at very least we can do away with the petty hatred and anger that causes us to strike out against those with whom we deal every day.

We should pray for those who suffer from the disasters of this world, but we should also pray for ourselves, that we will not contribute to the hatred that infects the world. And, when facing disasters beyond our control, we should remind ourselves of the truth:

> Nobility and strength are proven
> in times of crisis
> and so, too, are reason and love.

NOTE

1. Hazel E. Barnes, ed., *The Pessimist's Handbook* (Lincoln: University of Nebraska Press, 1964) 338–39.

Finding Joy in a Wrinkled Bed

The psalmist observes that it seems as if God has "disarranged all the sick person's bedding." What he means is this. Weakened by our disabilities, we all look for something on which we can rest. Good people find rest in their home, in their spouse, in their children, in the modest pleasures of their life, in their little piece of property, in the plants they have set in the ground with their own hands, in the buildings that their creativity has produced. Innocent people find their relaxation in things like these. But because God wants us to be in love only with eternal life, he mingles bitter elements with these innocent pleasures so that even in the midst of our joys we are not totally comfortable. God allows "the sheets on our bed to be wrinkled" so that we will not fall in love with this earthly stable instead of longing for the true home that awaits us in heaven. (*Commentary on Psalm 40*, 5)

There is no question that in many ways this life is a pain. The Hospice in which we live just now is like many other "Inns for Travelers" I have stayed in over the years. There always seemed to be something out of order. The people next door were noisy and disturbed my peace. At gatherings I was shamed by the "goings-on" of my wild compatriots. The meals disturbed my stomach. The bed disturbed my sleep.

I discovered over the years that there is no use in trying to find the perfect place to stay in this life because there is no "perfect" place. After all, we have been made for eternity, that grand land that lies just beyond the doors of death. How then could we be satisfied with anything less? Our beds now are indeed made uncomfortable by "wrinkled sheets." But why should this be so? Why can't we find a more comfortable bed as we wait our time to go home? If the promise of the psalmist is indeed true that "Yahweh will be his comfort on his bed of sickness; Yahweh will most carefully smooth out his bed when he is sick" (Psalm 41:3), why do we suffer so much in this life? Why do we meet such formidable obstacles, such arduous labor, so much distress from both our flesh and the world?

There is no question that as we twist and turn on our bed, entangling ourselves even more in its rumpled sheets, we feel like joining in the desperate cry of Augustine: "Can anyone unravel this twisted tangle of knots?" (*Confessions*, 2.10). Is it possible to find joy as we toss and turn on the unmade lumpy bed that is our life just now? If we were guilty of some great crime, we could understand our discomfort. If we were drunk last night, we could understand why this morning we have a hangover. Such discomforts are just "paying the piper" for a profligate life. We have dirtied our bed through our own fault.

If we have lived selfish, uncaring lives, we should not be surprised that we are now alone. No one cares for us because we have never cared for anyone else. After a lifetime of locking our door to all others, we cannot expect now that they will come to keep us company.

If we have just muddled through our work, if we have never dedicated ourselves to the job that was given us, it is no wonder that one day it is taken away from us. If we did not nurture our artistic and creative powers, there is no surprise that no harvest resulted from our lazy efforts.

But none of these things are true for most of us. We try to take care of ourselves, we try to love others, we try to do our work, but still the bed in which we must lie is rumpled by illness and loneliness and feelings of inadequacy. We cry out:

> We tried to live a healthy life; why then do we feel so bad now that we are old?
>
> We tried to spend our lives caring for family and friends; why have those we loved been taken away from us? Why are we now left alone?
>
> We spent so many years working hard; why now is no one interested in what we still have to give?

As we live out our days in this unkempt bed that is our life, we feel like crying out with Augustine in the midst of his own troubled life: "What torture! My soul turns and turns again, on its back and sides and belly, but the bed is always hard!" (*Confessions*, 6.16).

It is indeed difficult to understand why our bed-clothes (the fabric of our "life"), are so wrinkled. We are not "bad people." Indeed, a fitting epitaph for most of us would be: "At Least They Tried Their Best." And indeed we did! We tried our best to take care of our body and soul. We tried our best to reach out and embrace others with love. We tried our best to do a good job with the jobs given us. We tried our best to use our talents to bring something lovely or at least useful into the world. Why, then, are our sheets so wrinkled? Why does our life rankle? Augustine's words introducing this reflection suggest the answer that God would give to such questions. He would say to us:

> You did indeed *"try your best"* and because of this a grand life awaits you outside the doors of this Inn. Just now you must not be too attached to your room. Its defects, its troubles, its imperfections are motivation to move on. You should not let your troubles make you forget the wonderful things that are part of your life. With all that is sometimes wrong with this life, there are things in the present and in the future that should make you joyful.

Augustine had his share of troubles in life, but he never let them destroy his joy in the great good things he found in simply being alive. Even as the world seemed to be falling apart, he was able to say to his friends:

> The great good God has made us humans the loveliest orna-
> ments of the earth. Oh, it is true that we must someday die, but
> in our present living God has given us some wonderful things
> just perfectly fitted to us. . . . Above all, as we go through this
> life with its ups and downs, we have a promise from our lovely
> Lord that if we use well the wonderful things he has given us
> here on earth, we shall receive even greater things later on. We
> shall receive a peace beyond death and all the healing and glory
> that goes with it. We shall have the joy that comes from enjoy-
> ing again our earthly loves, embracing them as we are embraced
> in the arms of our loving, lovely God. And best of all: in the
> midst of our heavenly happiness we will suddenly realize that
> it is everlasting. We will know that finally and forever our joy
> will never end. (*City of God*, 12.13; 22.24)

As we continue to toss and turn in the "wrinkled" life that has been dealt to us, there are still many reasons to be joyful. All things considered, this life is "not too bad" and the life that awaits us outside this Hospice will not be bad at all.

Reaching for the Stars

The entire life of a good Christian is in fact an exercise of holy desire. You do not yet see what you long for, but the very act of desiring prepares you so that when God comes you may see and be utterly satisfied. (*Commentary on the First Letter of John*, 4.6.2)

The burden and blessing of being human is that we are born with a longing to be more than we are, to fly far above this earth and reach the stars. Deep down all of us desire to escape the narrow confines of our life and soar to something better, something truly wonderful, something truly good. It was this passion for "something better" that prompted Augustine to cry out: "In search of my God I poured out my soul above myself seeking to reach him" (*Commentary on Psalm 61*, 14).

The desire to "fly to the stars" is the passion that sends astronauts into space. It is the force that drives the artist to create the "perfect" work. It is the hunger that makes others explore new areas of knowledge: splitting the atom, understanding the mind, comprehending the mystery of love. Even when we are disabled and cannot walk (much less soar to the heavens), we look forward to the coming of those kind souls who will roll us out of our dark room to feel the warmth and light of the sun. We can no longer fly to the sky, but we can still look up and remember days past when such flight did not seem impossible. We sit and dream of future days when perhaps we will touch the sky and then go beyond. Augustine believed that human beings simply *must* go beyond their narrow selves if they are ever to achieve happiness. He told his friends: "As we restlessly seek happiness, we finally begin to realize that we must go beyond ourselves in order to be happy" (*Sermon 399*, 6). Like St. Paul, we try to forget our past and "strain towards what lies ahead" (Phil 3:13).

This effort to go beyond ourselves, to reach out for some star or other, can have a therapeutic effect even before we achieve the good desired. The longing for what is above and beyond can both stretch our capacity and purify it. As Augustine explains:

> What you long for you do not yet see, but by longing you stretch your spirit so that when what you are seeking has come, it finds sufficient space for it to fill. It is like wishing to fill your pocket with something or other. You see the size of the object and realize that the pocket is too narrow to contain it and so you stretch the pocket. This is what God does to us. By postponing our fulfillment in this life, he extends our longing and that longing stretches our spirit and increases its capacity. (*Commentary on the Epistle of John*, 4.6.2.)

Of course, we can also be stretched by longing for things less than ourselves (money, physical pleasure, etc.), but such earthy expansion prevents us from reaching above ourselves. We are like overweight people, unable to leap above that which is below us. We must go on a diet to lose the extra weight that has swollen us in a deathly way. We have been stretched by our longing but have become worse. Rather than reaching for the stars we have become embedded in the earth.

To want to reach the stars is a blessing, but it can also be dangerous when we reach too far beyond our capacities. It is natural for little children to want to explore new lands (the yard next door, the mysterious world "across the street"), but to do so on their own risks getting lost or being crushed by a rushing car. It is natural for us to search for "new experiences," but to do so through drugs or alcohol (reaching for exotic lands that exist only in our own mind) can cause us to lose ourselves in a vast darkness beyond reality. To overdose on fantasy may prevent us from ever returning to earth. To reach for a star that is an unattainable good or for a "death-star" that could destroy us, is a preview of hell. As Augustine observed: "All those who are enamored of something good that they cannot get should question themselves. Unable to attain the desired good, are they not tortured by their continuing obsession?" (*Commentary on Psalm 57*, #20).

There are various levels of success in this life for those who "reach for the stars," and happiness depends on being able to be satisfied with the life that has been given us. Some may make it to the planets, some have reached the moon, some only spin about the earth for a while and then disappear into the clouds. Perhaps all that most of us can do is stand in place and look up. To fly high we must be free of gravity. Those who fly to the highest heavens cannot be attached to any "thing" on earth. Only then can they reach out to the stars. As Augustine says, we reach out by our love and "our love becomes our weight" (*Confessions*, 13.9) drawing us faster and faster into the twinkling heaven above.

The dangers inherent in "reaching for the stars" are suggested by the various disasters that have occurred in the attempt to fly free of the earth into outer space. Some like the Challenger astronauts are destroyed in the ascent. In a terrible way they repeat the disaster of Icarus described in Greek mythology. In his attempt to fly free of the earth, Icarus reached for the stars higher and higher until his earthy wings were dissolved by the blazing heat of the sun.

Icarus's mistake was to believe too strongly in his own strength and on the strength of his wings. In a similar fashion, we cannot achieve heaven by depending on our own powers nor by presuming that the sustaining grace of God will protect us from our foolishness. God's grace will support us only as long as we use it wisely, not presuming that it will rescue us from every evil that our own stupidity creates. Like Icarus, we must not fly too close to the sun by pretending to be God, nor must we so immerse ourselves in this life that we dampen our untried wings by diving too close to the raging seas of this world.

The story of Icarus teaches us that it is dangerous for us to desire something that is far beyond what is possible for "cracked" human beings like you and me. Our dream ends in frustration because its object is beyond our capacity. Thus, sometimes we pretend to be gods but perish because we remain only human. Sometimes we reach out in love to clutch someone, but they are indifferent to our advances and we come back to the reality of our aloneness. Sometimes we pretend to be perfect, only to crash in despair when the weakness we have hidden even from ourselves suddenly surfaces in embarrassing ways.

When we reach for the stars imprudently, disaster can strike when we try to return (because sooner or later we must come back down to earth from our momentary ecstasy). We are then like the astronauts who perished when their ship Columbia perished on reentry. They had reached the heavens and for a time traveled among the stars but were shattered by the friction of the atmosphere when they tried to return to earth. So, too, with us in some of our more mundane adventures. We reach our desired "heaven," grasping that elusive star that we had pursued for so many years, but then the moment is over and we fall back to earth, once again deadened by the boredom of our ordinary humdrum life.

Such painful return to reality can occur in many different ways as we live out our lives in this Hospice. The young are sometimes overcome by the rapture of their first love, only to find that it is quickly over. Later on, after having achieved some eminence in the eyes of the world, their importance in the eyes of others diminishes and their days of living the "high life" are over. The experience of "crashing to earth" may come at the very end of life when you are informed that you must retire because you have become redundant (a fancy word meaning that "you are no longer useful to our company"). If you have no other prospects and nothing to "retire to" (a loving family, an interesting hobby, worthwhile volunteer work), you may suddenly realize that you have no more stars to reach for in this life, that now you must try to reach for the stars that twinkle beyond death if such there be.

Sadly, there are few in this life who in their search for the stars are able to mirror the success of Pioneer 10, the little space-ship *"that could."* As I write these words in 2003, it has already traveled 7.6 billion miles from earth and apparently is still on the move towards even more distant heavenly bodies. Like a great mystic reaching for heaven and beginning to live on the fringes of eternity, the little space-voyager is connected to the earth only by a slender thread of messages about what infinite space is like.

We should not be surprised that the messages of Pioneer 10 are now too faint to be heard here on earth. Even St. Augustine (*Confessions*, 9.10.23-24) and St. Paul (*2 Cor* 12:3-4) had difficulty putting into words their momentary mystical experiences. When we travel that far into the heaven of heavens, we are just too distant to be understood by those still trapped on earth. Hearing the voice of God commanding that we send his word to those below, we become like Jeremiah crying out in fear: "Ah, Lord God! I know not how to speak!" (Jer 1:6). If finally we are able to rise to the stars and go beyond to the heaven of heavens, our fragile line of communication with those below *must* be broken, not because of any defect in us or in those we have left behind but simply because we are too close to heaven and eternity to make much impact on the earth we have left behind.

The hopeful message of the Christian faith is that although our dream of reaching for the stars in this life may never be fulfilled, we have the power to reach for the stars that lie just beyond the limits of this life, the eternal stars that shine on God's City. Even more heartening is the assurance that God will help us on our journey, that with his help we will not "become" gods (as Icarus tried to become) but we will have a chance to be with God for all eternity.

Best of all, we need not worry about reaching the stars on our own. God has promised that our very "wanting" will open the door for him to come into our lives and lift us up to the heavens. In our trip to the eternal stars we will be carried by the strength of God, a strength that insures that our ascent (though sometimes difficult) will be successful in the end and that our landing will be surprisingly gentle. Then we will understand what God meant when he said: "You have seen for yourselves how I bore you up on eagle wings and brought you here to myself" (Exod 19:4).

Joyful Work

I recognized that there is nothing better than to be glad and to do
well in life. To eat and drink and enjoy the fruit of one's labor is for
every human being a gift of God. Indeed, there is nothing better
for humans than to rejoice in their work. (Eccl 3:12-13; 3:22)

A recent study of older Americans reported that eighty-
four percent preferred to continue working even though they no
longer needed work to support themselves. It seems that it was
not enough for them to "be"; they wanted to "do" something
worthwhile as long as they could. This desire for some sort of
"work" seems rooted in human nature. Augustine noted that
even before they sinned, humans were given a little work to do.
Commenting on the passage from Scripture, "And the Lord
God took the man whom he had made and placed him in Paradise to cultivate and guard it" (Gen 2:15), Augustine comments:

> That first man certainly was not being "condemned" to labor
> even before he sinned. Whatever delight comes from cultiva-
> tion of the earth must have been more powerfully present in
> that paradise as man enthusiastically helped God's creation
> bloom forth in joyful and abundant harvest. (*The Literal Mean-
> ing of Genesis,* 8.8.15)

Why were humans called upon to cultivate and guard nature? Paradise provided plenty of food and drink without the necessity of working for it. The only answer that makes sense is that God wanted human beings then and now to join in the development of the universe. The work of Creation occurred only once, but the work of developing Creation would go on till the end of time.

This development is driven by two aspects of God's providential care. God's providence working through nature brought it about that creation was given the ability to be molded into its various forms. It is this providence that gives plants the ability to grow, trees the ability to produce the wood and stones that can be hewn and formed to build cathedrals. It is through this same providence working in nature that humans were endowed with intelligence and freedom. It is under God's providence now working through the free choices of humans that they actually use their gifts to produce the crops and build the cathedrals and discover the oil to drive the engines and invent the computers which allow clods like me to write down thoughts like these (*The Literal Meaning of Genesis*, 8.9.17).

Augustine maintained that "any work that is done without fault or deception is a good work" (*The Work of Monks*, 12.14). These words were addressed to a group of monks who seemed to believe that manual labor was beneath them. Augustine's message to them was that being Christian (even being a monk) was not an excuse for avoiding a bit of physical labor. He adds that he himself would much prefer to work in the monastery garden than to spend his days settling the endless squabbles and disputes brought to him by the people of Hippo (*The Work of Monks*, 29.37).

Unfortunately, work is sometimes not as fulfilling as Augustine believed it could be. Many humans are forced into jobs that degrade rather than uplift, that frustrate rather than satisfy. In this post-paradisiacal world the work that we must do sometimes seems meaningless, the work of slaves rather than co-workers with God. Though Viktor Frankl suggests that frustration in work is due more to the individual than to the work,[1] some are unable to rise above the menial, servile, unappreciated work that crushes them. They cannot feel "good" about their work. All they can do is try to follow Augustine's advice "to bend lest you be broken" (*Catechizing the Uninstructed*, 14.20).

The effect of frustration at work may be debilitating but it is not as dangerous as its opposite: *work obsession*. When we are frustrated with the work we must do, at least we are not tempted to make it the sole reason for living. When we are obsessed with it, we are unable to see beyond it to anything else. Indeed, we define ourselves by our work, believing that when the work stops we will become nothing at all. Augustine warns that it is all well and good to dedicate ourselves to careers in farming or the military or the law or business, but every career, no matter how noble, is a "river of Babylon" rushing through time. In our enthusiasm for our work we must be careful lest its rushing waters sweep us away too (*Commentary on Psalm 136*, 2–3).

Because of our natural desire to work, to lose a job can be a traumatic experience. Unfortunately, to be gainfully employed is not entirely within our control. To get and do a job depends on the kindness of potential employers and the kindness of God giving us the strength and ability to do the work offered to us. Even those self-employed need customers. Even those drawn to the artistic life (painting, writing, etc.) need someone beyond themselves who appreciates what they have done. If we have spent our lives obsessed with work, losing a job, being forced to retire, having our self-proclaimed "great artistic creation" rejected, can be equivalent to killing us. We made our work our life and taking it away destroys us.

Even when we are not particularly obsessed with our work, losing a job (especially when it seems unlikely that we will find another) demands from us a new approach to our lives. Though not consumed by our work, we have gotten used to it. It gave focus to our life. It gave a reason to get up in the morning. It gave us a special community of co-workers who shared with us that one-third of the day that was spent at work. The times at the water-cooler or coffee-maker or lunch table were as much the places of our lives as the dinner table with our family. The friendly (and sometimes unfriendly) gossip about boss and co-workers was an area of knowledge that we could not get anywhere else.

When all this is taken away (even when we give it away voluntarily), a gap opens in our lives that demands to be filled in some way. For some with nothing to do the great event becomes waiting for the daily paper to arrive to learn what others are doing. At loose ends, some spend their days following their spouse around and driving them crazy. Losing their job for one reason or another, they seem now to have become vegetables, existing in a vacuum created by their absent career and having no thought or energy to discover something else to do with their lives.

If one goes into a "blue funk" after losing a job, it is unlikely that they will ever find another; indeed, it is unlikely that they will ever move beyond their apathetic paralysis. This is a shame because it prevents them from discovering the most important tasks of their lives, tasks that only they can do, tasks that can only be given away, not taken away. These are tasks that are more important than anything else they have accomplished in their earthly careers. They are more important because they determine whether they will be a success in eternity. These tasks are two:

1. To make ourselves worthy of being vessels of God;
2. To allow God to work through us to bring good to others.

When we are in the midst of our over-active lives, it is sometimes difficult to remember that our importance comes not from *doing* things but from *being* what we are, vessels of Almighty God in this ever-moving life. Our primary task is to make ourselves the reflection of God that he wants us to be. Admittedly, it is a difficult task, a task which made Augustine cry out: "My work is myself. I have become for myself a land of difficulty and too much sweat" (*Confessions,* 10.16.25). If we have begun the work of polishing God's image in ourselves, we can then turn to the work that St. Paul described: "Each should please their neighbor by doing them good and building up their spirit" (Rom 15:3). If we can do nothing else for those around us, we can try to make their lives a bit happier. Even if we cannot actively "do them good," we can try to "build up their spirit" by not tearing them down, by not getting in the way of their happiness.

And let's face it, we are not agents of joy for those around us all the time. On some days we are like that little fellow that was featured in the "Little Abner" comic strip of times past, the little fellow who walked down the sunny streets with a storm-cloud over his head, raining on everyone else's life. To be sure, on some days we don't feel like instruments of joy. But even on those days we can "build up the spirits" of others by not forcing our gloom on them. If all we can do on some days is to chant a dirge, we should have the charity to keep our mouth shut when company comes. This is not merely pietistic "do gooding." It is letting the divine love of the Christ who lives in us shine on the lives of others. This indeed is a worthwhile work. It is a lovely labor because it is a labor of love, and it is by such labors that someday we will come to see the face of the Lord of love.

No matter how great our accomplishments may be on earth, they are all passing. We and the angels are the only part of creation that will exist forever, and all that we will take with us into eternity will be what we have done *to* ourselves and done *for* others. There is nothing wrong in trying to find other more mundane work to fill out our days but in doing that work we should follow the advice of St. Paul: "Whatever you do, work at it with your whole strength and do it for the Lord rather than for human beings" (Col 3:23-24).

NOTE

1. Viktor Frankl, *The Doctor and the Soul* (New York: Alfred A. Knopf, 1986) 118.

A Life of No Importance

If you stay in any Inn for Travelers in this world, sooner or later you begin to ask the question, "Why am I here?" The same question arises in this Hospice that is the world in which we live just now. It is hard to discover any meaning when you are living the life of a transient (as we all are). Over the years I have stayed in many motels and hotels (usually while attending a philosophy conference), and I cannot remember feeling any importance about my stay. I was there only because the conference would look good on my résumé or to deliver a paper. Most of the presentations were serious, but I cannot remember any of them (including my own) having a long-lasting impact.

Of course, I derived some "meaning" from giving the paper, and there was a certain feeling of importance that came from others believing that my thoughts were worth being part of the program. But even then my sense of importance was somewhat dampened when my paper was given during the last session and the audience was sitting with their hats and coats on ready to leave at a moment's notice. They, like me, were anxious to get "going" and return to the familiar home where those they loved were waiting. None of them seemed to rejoice in the simple fact that they were in a pleasant Hospice, a temporary but comfortable Inn for Travelers.

And so it is with us as we live out our allotted days in this world, this place for those who are passing through. Since our stay is not for a weekend but for our whole life, and since we have had no experience of a life that awaits us outside the doors when we "check-out," we may not be terribly anxious to leave even though we find it hard to discover any importance in staying longer. The motel may be comfortable (as this life often is), the staff may be accommodating, there may be tasks to be accomplished, and we may be surrounded by some we love, but even so, it is hard to see any great significance in our existence as transients. In the midst of such a quickly moving life, there is a natural tendency to ask: "Does my life 'mean' anything or is it just a 'life of no importance'?"

The older I get the more I become convinced that Viktor Frankl is correct in saying that our most persistent desire as human beings is to have our lives "mean something!"[1] It is not enough for us to live, we must "make sense" of our life, to become convinced that our life has some importance, that there is something in us that justifies our existence, some reason why *we* exist rather than someone more noble.

There are many living things in this Hospice (plants and animals, bugs and bacteria), but I as a human being seem to be the only animal who raises the question: "Does my life have any importance?" It is true that some animals may "stake out their territory" in their animal way by leaving their "mark" on a convenient tree and they may start families in their animal way, but it is difficult to see that they seek territory or offspring so that they can become important. They don't worry about the meaning of life; they just live it. A sick animal is a sad animal. A caged animal is an unhappy animal. An animal deemed unimportant does not seem to be upset by the designation. Humans are quite different. To live a truly "human" life, we must at least try to find some meaning in our existence.

The search can be quite painful, and we may be tempted to try to deaden or eliminate our unfulfilled desire, believing that a thoughtless "unexamined" life is better than a discouraging examined life. We may try to find meaning through factors outside ourselves. Some will seek meaning through their work; others, through being loved. But neither of these methods answers the question: "Why am I, IN AND OF MYSELF, important?" Meaning from work comes from what I *DO;* meaning from the love of others comes from what others *DO TO ME.* Neither reveals any special meaning or special importance in being who *I AM.* Moreover, both work and love are fleeting. Work will someday be finished; a loved one may die. We will then discover that absence does not always make a heart grow fonder; it may cause one's life to founder. If we have based the meaning of our lives on being loved by another, when that person dies the reason for our continuing existence may die with them.

Even a great and glorious love that is now past cannot give us a feeling that our life means something now. It may give us a fond memory of our love, that "indeed there was a time in the past when someone cared about me," but it does not ease our loneliness right now. The elderly rocking away their solitary lives on the porch of a retirement home may remember warmly the days when they were young and vigorous, raising children, dancing with loved ones, playing with friends, days when they seemed to be important to so many people. But such reminiscence does not take away the pain of now being alone, being cared for and cared about by someone who is paid to do so. It is no wonder that suicide is sometimes embraced by such solitary souls. When no one cares about you *for* yourself, it is easy to give up caring *about* yourself.

To accomplish the difficult task of living and dying nobly, I must become convinced that "in and of myself" I have a special dignity, a unique importance in the scheme of things. Strengthened by such belief, I may still not be able to control the times of my life, but I can at least control my attitude towards them. As Augustine said: "We make our times" (*Sermon 80,* 8), and we do so through the manner in which we face them. Admittedly, considering the erratic "ups" and "downs" of daily existence, it is hard sometimes to have a positive opinion about ourselves. When we are shoved out of the way trying to get on a bus, when people look through us and beyond us as we talk to them, when we have tried to work diligently in our job only to be declared no longer useful, when our spouse seems too busy to spend time with us, when our children no longer seem to like us, when at parties no one seems interested in who we are and what we are doing, on such occasions we may come to believe that we are "of no account" because no one seems to take account of us.

In such situations all we can do is try to get beyond our humiliating experience and reach out to our faith. If we are Christians, there are great reasons for believing in our unique importance in the universe. It was because of his belief in Christ and the Providence of God that Augustine was able to confidently proclaim: "Considering that in God's plan for this universe not even one leaf on a tree is wasteful, it is not possible that any human being be without importance" (*On Freedom of the Will*, 3.23.66). It was that belief that led him to assert that we human beings (along with the angels) are the loveliest part of creation (*City of God*, 19.13). We cannot despair of ourselves if we believe his assurance that "you are made in the image of God and he who made you human became human himself for your sake. The blood of God's only Son was poured out for you so that you, all of you, might become God's children" (*Commentary on Psalm 32/2*, #4). Indeed, in our power to discover the truth and choose the good we are the most perfect reflections of God in the universe (*Sermon 43*, 3).

But granted that human beings are reflections of God, why am *I* so important, considering that there are so many others more gifted, more virtuous than I? The answer is that I am unique. I live a life that only I can live. I experience the world from my own special perspective and the world experiences me as something quite different from all other human beings. The reflection of God in me is different from all others, and I must be important in his eyes, otherwise he would not have called me into existence. I am important because I am important to God. The brilliance of God filtering through my life may sometimes be quite dim but it comes through me in a distinctively original way.

As I write these words, I remember my growing up years in Philadelphia. On the ledge of our kitchen window, my mother had gathered bottles of various shapes and sizes. She had filled them with clear water that she had tinted in different colors: some blue, some green, some red, some orange, some yellow. When the sun rose, the light would shine through the bottles creating rainbows on the floor and wall of the room. All of the bottles were filled with the same water (and in that they shared a common nature) and even though they were different in size and shape, the sun seemed to shine through them equally well. I asked my mother, "Why keep that tiny bottle that is filled with the red water? It seems out of place considering the great size and dramatic shape of the other bottles." My mother answered: "It is tiny to be sure, but if we did not have it, there would be no red radiance shining in the room."

Now I can understand why God created me especially. With every other human being I am filled with the same substance, a substance that allows the Divine Light to shine through me into this world. Small I may be and cracked I certainly am, but without me the universe would be lacking that special color of God's presence that my unimpressive life provides. The rainbow of creation would be incomplete because there would be no color, "Donald." On days when I feel dull and unimportant, I think of that and am consoled.

NOTE

1. Viktor E. Frankl, *The Doctor and the Soul* (New York: Vintage Books, 1986) xvi.

Bringing Christ to My World

In my travels in this life, usually to meetings of philosophers, my activities during my stay were always pointed towards the effect they would have on my life once I left the hotel. Indeed, the very reason why I was at the meeting was to show that I was a member of the club, a practicing philosopher among others of my ilk, and to convey that fact to the great world beyond the doors of my temporary residence, the world that controlled my promotions and salary. When I delivered a formal paper to the ten or twenty hardy souls who by mistake had wandered into my lecture, the sparse attendance never bothered me because I knew that my name would appear in the program to be read by those beyond the doors who hopefully might come to believe that I did something worthwhile in my days of traveling.

Now that I have retired from my career as a teacher, I find myself asking myself: "What am I supposed to do now? What can I do now that will insure a place in the City of God once I 'check-out' of this Inn for Travelers?" Unfortunately I don't think it will be enough to point out to the gatekeepers that while in this Hospice I went to philosophy conventions, nor that I tried to teach philosophy to the unwilling for forty years. Such information did not even impress the taxi drivers who took me to the airport after my philosophy meetings were over. It is unlikely that such declarations will have much effect on those who (in the next life) guard the entrances to God's

City. What then can I do now to impress them? What can I do now that in God's eyes will seem worthwhile?

The answer given by my Christian faith is that (even in retirement) I must do my best to bring Christ to the world that I face each day. In some way or other I must try to imitate Mary, the mother of Jesus. Like her, I must be a "Christ-Bearer," bringing Christ to that little piece of reality, that little room in this Hospice where I live out my life. Augustine put it this way to the people in his church: "The mother Mary bore Jesus in her womb; let us bear him in our hearts. The virgin became pregnant through the Incarnation of Christ; let our hearts become pregnant with his presence through our Faith in him" (*Sermon 189*, 3).

Mary's example is indeed instructive. She bore witness to that second life living in her long before the wombed Christ could be perceived directly by others. John the Baptist was the only exception. While still deep in the womb of his mother Elizabeth, he felt the presence of the hidden Jesus and jumped for joy. In a similar fashion, if we could make the Divine Jesus live in us as powerfully as he once lived in Mary, then we would be well on the way to bringing him to our world. He would leap from our life just as he once sprang from the womb of Mary. But first we must say "Yes" to him just as Mary said "Yes" to the angel when she received into her womb the Incarnate God.

What does saying "Yes" mean for us? Is this just a pious expression with no content? It certainly does not mean going around all day saying "Yes, Jesus!" and doing nothing more. What it does mean is saying "Yes, Jesus, I want you to live in me!" and then going out and doing something about it. It means trying to "be" Jesus for every person we meet. To be a Christ-Bearer in this world does not demand that we perform miracles, merely that we try to make the best of the day that is given us while helping others to make the best of theirs.

The example of the young maiden Mary shows us that we cannot avoid the duty of "proclaiming the Lord" by claiming that we are not talented enough or that we are too crippled by life to do any effective "proclaiming." My friend Marion was a proof of this. She was an accomplished artist and, as I type these words, I see before me the last painting she did before she died. It is a picture of Christ as he looked just after he heard Pilate's terrible words: "Nothing more can be done!" I suggested to Marion that these words would be a good title for her painting because they said something about her suffering as well as the suffering of Christ. Crippled by an unsuccessful back operation, she had heard those same words from her doctors when she asked for some relief from the pain. They told her: "We are sorry, Marion. Nothing more can be done to relieve your pain because you are not terminal."

Marion had to live out the rest of her days in unremitting pain, but it did not stop her from painting. She painted this last picture mostly from her bed, though sometimes she would work propped up on a crutch until the pain got too bad. The portrait that resulted is especially striking because of the eyes. Instead of the dark eyes you would normally expect in a man of Christ's human lineage, the eyes are bright blue. The explanation for the unusual color is simple. One day Marion, after a series of unsuccessful attempts to get the eyes as she wanted them, dragged herself and the painting into the bathroom. Standing in pain before the mirror, she propped the unfinished canvas on the sink and painted her *own* eyes into the face of Jesus. Thus, now as I sit looking at the portrait of the swarthy face of the suffering Jesus, I see looking back at me the pain-filled blue, blue eyes of my friend Marion.

I think Jesus is pleased with his picture because it symbolizes the union he would like to have with every human being. He wants to live in us so powerfully that he can look through our eyes and see the world we face each day. He wants to live so powerfully in us that others will look in our eyes and see the eyes of Jesus Christ looking back. If he truly lives in me to that degree, then I am certain that he will not be *able* to condemn me on Judgment Day because he will look at the sin-weathered face of "Donald" and see looking back at him his own eyes: the eyes of Jesus Christ.

There is no question that it is not easy to bring Christ into our daily life to that degree, but he expects that we will at least try. Augustine took seriously the story of the servant who hid away the wealth given him by the master for investment (cf. Luke 19:11ff.). Although he himself would have dearly loved a quiet life of reflection, he felt the force of the Jesus hiding inside him. He cried out:

> Lord, you frighten me! You will not allow me not to preach. You demand from me what you gave me. You gave me my talents because you want to profit from them. You don't want them hidden away in some secret place. (*Sermon 125*, 8)

Whatever our talents may be, Christ wants us to bring him into our world. When we try to do that, we give him an opportunity to bury himself deeper and deeper into our very selves. In seeking to convert the world, we transform ourselves into vessels of God.

As we try to live our ordinary lives as Christ would live them, we should not despair at our failings. We have not yet become Jesus Christ. We are still in flux and so, too, is he in us. He is still fighting like the good doctor he is to stabilize our vital signs. He is still fighting to become more of our lives. He is still fighting to purge our lives of their weakness so that we can begin to live in strength in him. Our task just now is to say "Yes" to his wish to be present in us. If we do only that to the best of our ability, then whatever else happens to us, "We will have proclaimed the Lord!"

This is the only work we need do to make our lives worthwhile in the eyes of God.

Holy Indifference

When Christ told us to be detached from this world, he was not telling us that we must give up everything that gives us joy, things like good health, being in love, possessions, fulfilling our ambitions. All he was saying was that we should use all of these great good things in life in the right way.

His command to love God above all and our neighbor as ourselves means that there is nothing wrong in taking care of ourselves or in reaching out in love towards the rest of creation. God decided that we should work out our salvation *through* the good use of created things, not *in spite of them*. His original plan was that this would be easy. Humans were created in an earthly paradise where all things were in their proper place and got along just fine. This grand plan failed, not because nature suddenly became evil, but because humans made bad decisions.

Because this world is still good, it remains virtuous for us to take care of our health, to protect nature, to care for our pets, to love other humans. There is nothing wrong in becoming "attached" to our things or our loves as long as the "glue" that holds us to them is not so strong that we cannot lose them without perishing. This can happen. In our present weakened condition, we can become so *attached* to the good things in our life that we no longer have the strength to become *detached* when they begin to interfere with our eternal destiny.

Spiritual writers speak of this saving detachment as a "holy indifference" whereby we subordinate all persons, objects, and conditions of life to our pursuit of God. Unquestionably such holy indifference is difficult to achieve. Sometimes it comes only when (despite our great plans) we lose control of our lives. When Fr. John Neuhaus was close to death from illness, he wondered why he no longer seemed afraid to die. He analyzed this surprising indifference by admitting: "It probably had less to do with holiness than with my knowing that there was nothing I could do about it one way or the other."[1] I can't say that I have shared Father Neuhaus' battle with death, but I have had one or two bouts with debilitating illness. At such times I was very comfortable in "letting go," in letting things happen, in not worrying about the future, in letting others take care of me, letting others worry about me. It struck me then that just as we put ourselves in the hands of a kind nurse at such times, so in the midst of our days of health and vigor we should try to develop some form of holy indifference, putting ourselves in the hands of the provident God who certainly loves us and will do his best to fulfill our wishes.

The trick is to "wish" for nothing on earth too much, to "wish" only that we will be faithful to the life that God has planned for us. But, as I have said, it not an easy thing to do when we are in the flourishing prime of our lives and have come to believe that we can control our destiny. When things are going good for us, we tend to plan and worry about the future, to make lists of things we think we really need in order to be happy: the perfect place to live, someone who loves us, the praise of others (and perhaps their envy) when we are successful. At such moments we forget the truth that: "the less you want, the less you need" and that it is our "wanting" that causes most of our distress. It truly is crazy because as Augustine noted:

> Who has ever reached everything they hoped for? When you come close to grasping the object of your desire, it immediately

starts losing its charm. You begin to hope for other things, other attractions. And as soon as you obtain them they too begin to lose their charm. (*Sermon 125*, 11)

One important *caveat* in our supposedly "noble" pursuit of holy indifference is that we cannot use it as an excuse for ignoring our responsibilities in this world. To turn our back on the things of this world is neither virtuous nor possible. What the saints called holy indifference is not a lack of concern or apathy towards what is happening to us or around us. There is indeed a danger in immersing ourselves in worldly affairs but we must be involved in the trivialities of the day if we are to make Christ real to our sometimes trivial times (*Letter 95*, 2).

Despite the dangers, we must continue to be involved in the world in which we live. As Peter wrote to the Christians of the first century, we must "put our gifts at the service of one another, each in the measure we have received" (1 Peter 10). This is what the great saints did. In the midst of their struggle for holy indifference, Aquinas continued writing, Ignatius Loyola continued his missionary work, and the "Little Flower" (St. Thérèse of Lisieux) kept on doing the laundry for her sick sisters. For them holy indifference did not mean giving up the world. It just meant that they were not "attached."

Such detachment or intelligent indifference is necessary for us in order to clarify our vision so that we can see the true depth and length of our existence. It is hard to have any comprehension of the heavens above if our attention is consumed by the here and now. We must look up and look out to see the eternal destiny before us and begin to make proper decisions about the way to get there successfully. While giving things that are "other" than God their true value, we must be ready to separate ourselves from them, if we are to be free to move on.

Such holy indifference is the only way to have some semblance of peace of mind in the midst of the turmoil of our lives. To be at peace we must somehow develop the submissiveness of the humble clay, ready to have our future determined and molded by the powerful hands of the divine craftsman who controls our lives and wants only the best for us. Indeed, the secret of mental health in this Hospice is to not have our happiness depend absolutely and exclusively on things we cannot control—our loves, our health, our possessions, earthly honors or success. And (as Augustine advises) the time to develop this "freeing" outlook is when life is going well, when the world seems to be supplying all that we need to be happy. That is the time when we must learn to "let go of it before it lets go of us" (*Sermon 125*, 11).

Augustine believed that this was one of the central messages delivered by the example of Christ. He writes:

> Jesus chose to endure with us all the pains of being human so that we might not seek our happiness in earthly goods nor be afraid of becoming unhappy when we must give them up. (*On Catechizing the Uninstructed*, 40)

We must be sufficiently free of the things and people of this world so that if and when we lose them we are able to say with Job: "The LORD has given, the LORD has taken away; as it pleased the LORD, so has it happened; may the name of the LORD be blessed" (Job 1:21). This indeed is holy indifference because it is an indifference that will eventually make us holy.

NOTE

    1. Richard John Neuhaus, *As I Lay Dying: Meditations Upon Returning* (New York: Basic Books, 2002) 155.

Waiting for God to Call

Over the years, when I was forced to travel far from home (usually attending a philosophy conference at one hotel or another), I sometimes got an overpowering urge to speak to someone from outside the walls, a loved one or a friend or, indeed, anyone who would connect me with the life beyond the narrow confines of the Inn for Travelers where I lived just then.

The urge usually occurred at night when all the activities had ceased. Then I was left to myself and a television, telling stories of fantasy worlds that had little relationship to the real world that I personally would experience once I exited the Inn. The flickering screen presented no interviews with those who had already departed the transient life of the Inn. There was no sage advice from anyone who could describe to me what waited for me when I left. There was no guidance about how I should live out the rest of my days before I exited.

On nights such as these I sometimes looked at the phone, hoping for it to ring. But usually there were no messages from those beyond the walls. All messages seemed to be "inter-office" or "inter-room"—sometimes from compatriots wishing to re-hash the events of the day, events that seemed to have little impact on my life once I left the Inn. The calls from room-service asking what they could do for me were gracious but unsatisfying. They never presumed to say that they could serve me once I was called to the world beyond the walls of the Inn.

Sometimes I took the initiative and called outside, looking for someone who would speak to me about the wide, wide world that awaited me beyond the walls. Sadly I could not make the connection. I got a busy signal or a cold voice saying that I was calling a wrong number. When I did finally get through and was able to talk to one or other of my loves, I was filled with joy. Although I could not leave the Inn just then (I still had business to accomplish), I now knew that there was a someone who loved me waiting for me when my time came to exit.

As I live out my days in this Inn for Travelers that is the place where I will live until I die, in the quiet of the night I sometimes wish that the phone would ring and the voice on the other end would say: "Hello, this is God calling and I am waiting to receive you when your earthly business is over."

Once immersed in the "busyness" of the day, the need to hear God disappeared. I forgot about talking to God, so busy was I talking to other wanderers about the trivialities of our lives here at the Inn. When night came, the urge to talk to God and have God talk to me became strong again. I called and called only to get a busy signal or a wrong number or the information desk saying: "We are sorry but that number seems to be unlisted."

In a new T.V. show called "Joan of Arcadia," God is depicted as coming in the form of ordinary people to speak to a young girl. Her reaction of disbelief is to be expected. After all, why would God want to speak to a teenager (much less me) face to face and why would he come in the guise of the "ordinary"? If he came to me as he came to Moses, as a burning light, it might be easier to believe. If he knocked me off my high-horse and blinded me for a while as he did to Paul, I might believe. But in the stream of ordinary events and ordinary people passing by, it is hard to hear God calling to me.

Why is it that God does not call to us in some dramatic way that would *force* us to believe in the wonderful world beyond the doors of this life? Perhaps it is for our own good. The mystery of living in a world of the unknown draws us into the future towards the place where God lives, to that place which is our only home. I can see the reasonableness of such a plan. Even in this life, if all those I loved and desired were here with me in my room at the Inn, I would have no urge to leave. That would be terrible because none of us are meant to live in this Inn for Travelers forever. We were meant to spend some time here (hopefully doing some good) and then go home by exiting once and for all through the doors to the outside, the doors that we call death.

In living in a world where God is not shouting at us, a world that reflects God, that hints at God, we will better appreciate the eternal day when God will reveal himself face to face once and forever. This certainly is a better alternative than having God come to visit us "every once in a while" in this life and ignore us when we exit. The dramatic appearance of God to some of the saints was not the basis for their hope. No one in history has existed in a permanent ecstatic state in this life. Those who have had a mystical experience, an experience where God was present to them and even talked to them, only had such experiences for a moment. The great Moses once stood face to face with God in a burning bush, but it was only for a few hours. Very quickly he had to return back down the mountain to the dark confusion of the world below.

One thing is certain: having God call on a regular basis would not change our lives that much. It did not stop Adam and Eve (after walking and talking with God in paradise) from going their own way and then hiding in fright once they realized their mistake. Seeing God on the mountain did not prevent Moses from doubting. It did not insure that he would continue to see God face to face. The best he could manage thereafter apparently was to see only the back parts of God as he rushed by (*The Literal Meaning of Genesis*, 12.27.55). Seeing and talking to Jesus did not stop the apostles from running away from him when things got difficult. It did not stop Judas from betraying him.

Our mistake in waiting for God to call us in some dramatic way is that this is not the way God speaks to us in this life. God does not call to us from someplace "out there." He speaks to us from deep inside. As Augustine says, he is more "inward than our most inward selves" (*Commentary on Psalm 118/22*, 6). We carry him with us in this life and he is constantly whispering to us as we go through our days.

But if God calls to us from inside our own "self," why is it that we have such difficulty hearing him? Perhaps it is because we are like a person in a hotel room trying to make a call while deafened by the rock-music coming from the neighboring suite. We are unable to hear the whispering voice of God because we are deafened by the cacophony of our surroundings. In some way or another we must be like Zacchaeus, climbing above the noisy crowd to hear the Lord (*Sermon 174*, 3–6). It was the loud busyness of his everyday life that prompted Augustine to pray:

> Look Lord, I would like to sit down with you and have a little talk. Let others who deny your truth bark and howl as much as they want. Let them drive themselves crazy with their own noise. I will try to get them to shut up and then wait to be touched by your words. But if they won't quiet down at least may you keep talking loudly to me, Lord. "Do not be silent to me" (Psalm 27:1). Speak here inside me. I shall leave all the fussing folks outside, blowing on the ground and stirring up dust into their own eyes. I will go into my own little room deep inside my heart and sing love songs to you. (*Confessions*, 12.16.23)

Augustine realized that such concentration on God would not be easy. Conscious of his own weakness, he prayed:

> Say anything you wish but heal my ears so that I may pay attention to what you say. Heal my eyes so that I may see you when you beckon. Heal my stupidity so that I can recognize you when you come. Tell me where to look to see you and then I will hope that I will have the strength to do what you want of me. (*Soliloquies*, 1.3 and 1.5)

This last prayer is especially important for all of us because sometimes the reason why we do not hear God calling is because we are afraid of what we might hear. We disconnect the phone, lest the voice on the other end tells us something about ourselves that we have been trying to avoid. As Augustine admits:

> O Lord of truth, you are ready and willing to answer any question asked. And you always answer our questions clearly but not all of us can hear so clearly. Everybody asks you for answers they wish to hear but they do not always hear what they wish. Your best servant is the one who does not always expect to hear the answer he desires, but always ends up desiring whatsoever he hears from you. (*Confessions*, 10.26.37)

To hear God in this life we must truly "want" to hear him and be ready to accept the message that comes from him. The message will come from deep inside, telling us what is right and what is wrong with our lives. There will usually not be a great moment of ecstasy with it. We will not see "heaven." Angels will not appear, but the voice of conscience will be indeed the voice of God trying to prepare us for the happy life that is beyond the doors of this Inn for Travelers. But to hear the voice we need to follow Augustine's advice:

> Let us leave a little room for reflection, room too for silence. Enter into yourself, and leave behind all noise and confusion. Look within yourself. See whether there be some delightful hidden place in your consciousness where you can be free of noise and argument, where you need not be carrying on your disputes and planning to have your own stubborn way. Hear the word in quietness, that you may understand it. (*Sermon 52*, 22)

A Room with a View

How strange it is that the various parts of the flea are marvelously fitted together in an orderly fashion while the life of the human being appears surrounded and disturbed by the chaos of countless disorders! We are sometimes like those who examine a vast inlaid pavement but can see only the outline of one tile. With such a narrow focus we find it easy to condemn the creator of the floor. Our myopic vision makes us think that the tiles are disorganized because we cannot see how they fit together in one beautiful whole. This is what happens to empty-headed humans who, because of their feeble minds, are unable to appreciate the order of reality. They think that the whole universe is disordered because the one little stone which they have made their whole life displeases them. (*On Order,* 1.1.2)

—

This quote from Augustine makes me think of an ant crawling laboriously on its little feet across the floor of the Sistine Chapel, hopefully waving its antenna from side to side seeking some sort of nourishment, some sort of excitement, something beyond that "next tile" that is its future, that "next tile" that seems no different from the present boring tile that defines its life. I can imagine that little nearsighted ant praying for something *different*, even if it is only to be squashed flat by the feet of hurrying pilgrims busy about their own rocks, those narrow pebbles that constitute their history and promise to be their only future.

The problem with the poor ant plodding across its tile floor and the poor "US" plodding through our days in this Inn is that our vision is often too confined to see the reality of our eternal lives. Like the ant, it is hard for us to see even the beauty of the whole floor we traverse, our time on earth, and, as far as being able to raise our eyes to see the beauty above, the eternity that awaits us, why that is just impossible! The task is beyond the capacity of our poor myopic two-dimensional imagination. This can happen to us if we live too long in this Hospice. We may become so accustomed to it that we stop looking any farther to find our destiny. We narrow our focus to such an extent that we cannot see anything beyond the little toys gathered in our room. We close the blinds to the outside sun, despairing of ever seeing anything of interest beyond the here and now.

That's why it's nice to have a "room with a view," a room where we are able to see something of the beauty beyond our little assigned space and even beyond the Inn itself, a room where we are able to sit on the balcony and converse with our fellow INN-Mates as we enjoy the fresh breezes and brilliant colors of the world beyond the walls of our narrow temporary residence. In my days of traveling and staying in various hotels I always wanted such a "room with a view." I discovered that, no matter how exotic the facilities, I soon got tired of the amenities inside and sought distraction outside. I wanted to take a walk in the fresh air (to get free of all the hot air inside), to see the sights in the unlimited world beyond the doors, to meet new friends.

Even when the great outdoors was truly great, more often than not my under-budgeted convention trips prevented me from seeing it. My room was usually on an inner court where the only view I had was of the foibles and follies of those across the way who with raised shades and open windows exposed their mixed-up lives to anyone who cared to look. But soon such little dramas became no more stimulating than a daytime soap opera without the advertisements.

Such confinement, such narrowness of vision, can be deadening when it occurs in our lives. We need to see distances to keep our sanity. When I was teaching college in Miami, someone in charge of the public schools decided that new schools would be more efficient, safe, and environmentally sound if they were built as concrete boxes with good air-conditioning and heating but no windows to the outside. It was soon discovered that in such schools the mental health of students and staff suffered. Day after day they could see nothing beyond the dull walls of their slowly dying life. They had little to look at and soon felt that they had little to look forward to.

The same thing can happen to us if we spend our days in this Hospice in a room with no view, if we cannot look forward to anything beyond the walls of our temporary shelter, if we look at the rooms and places in this Inn and say to ourselves:

> This is the place where I must live out my life. There is nothing beyond to look forward to. My death will not be the beginning of any new life; it will just be an end of this one, leaving nothing behind but my few remains to be disposed of in an environmentally safe way.

It is terrible to go through the various times of our lives in a room with no view of what is beyond the present moment. I am told that young people sometimes commit suicide because they see nothing to look forward to. Workers who cannot see a time when they can work less sometimes end up being crushed by their work. Parents with sick children who cannot look forward to seeing them grow and prosper, carry a sorrow that only they know because their "room" has no view of a better future for those they love.

The strange thing about this lack of vision is that everyone has the possibility of developing their own "room with a view." There is no special reservation necessary because the room is created inside the "self" by an optimistic spirit that looks forward to the rest of life here and the life that awaits beyond the doors of this Hospice. The trouble is that it is hard to do this if we are surrounded by those who are satisfied with the narrow confines of their own little rooms. It is hard to have long-range vision in a kingdom of the nearsighted. Here, as in every case of something good happening to us in this Hospice, we need a little help from our friends.

Here I think of one of my friends who was a great help in my getting an appreciation of a life that is eternal. He led a graceful life to old age, keeping his humor along the way. He complained a bit about not being able to remember what happened yesterday, but his memory of the distant past was clear and true. I believe that he was just as farsighted in looking into the future. As he came to the end of his days in this Inn, he insisted on being part of the planning for his own funeral: who should be invited, who should preach, and so forth. On the day before his death he woke from an afternoon nap with a start and called out to those in the next room: "Am I dead yet?" It was not a cry of fear but of anticipation because he had a "room with a view" and could already see something of the grandeur that awaited him beyond the doors of this Hospice.

The old Augustine on the eve of his retirement seemed to express a similar vision when he wrote to a friend:

> In this life we are all going to die someday and that last day of life is uncertain for all of us. In infancy we look forward to our childhood. In our childhood we look forward to being adolescents. In adolescence we look forward to being young adults. As young adults we look forward to middle age. In middle age we look forward to old age. But when we are old there is nothing more to look forward to in this life. After old age there is no other age. (*Letter 213*, 1)

Taken at face value the reflection is somewhat depressing, presenting a picture of a person who wanders from room to room in this Inn looking for something more only to find that when he reaches the end there is nothing more to see. It is the picture of a human being who is condemned to stay in an Inn for Travelers that has "no rooms with a view" because there is nothing to view beyond the dark walls of this life.

But Augustine did not mean his words to be depressing. The point that he was making in this letter to his friend is that when we reach the end of this life, when it is obvious that our time in this Inn is running out, truly there is nothing more to look forward to *here in the Inn*. But there is much to look forward to if we have lived in a "room with a view" that gave us a vision of what awaits us beyond the doors of the Inn.

At one time in his life (before his conversion to Christ) Augustine experienced the agony of those who cannot achieve such vision. In his twenties he had no clear idea of any life beyond the doors of this life. But with his conversion a window opened. Through faith he was given a "room with a view" and through that window he was able to see the infinite spaces beyond the walls of this Hospice. Through faith he was able to look through that window and see the eternal future that awaited him. Through hope he was able to see that it was indeed possible for him to go through the doors to the land where indeed there "was nothing to look forward to" because all that he could hope for was forever present to him.

His faith had given him a "room with a view" and, seeing the future that awaited him in the great wide world outside this life, he was able to live out his remaining days in this Hospice in happiness and hope, making his own the sentiments of the psalmist:

> "I will be glad and exult in you; I will sing praise to your name, Most High" (Psalm 9:2-3). I will rejoice and exult but no longer in the days left to me here. I will rejoice but not in the pleasures of loving caresses nor in the wonderful tastes and sweet scents and soothing sounds of a life that must fade away. Nor will I exult in the shimmering beauty of the colors of these days

on earth nor in the vanity of human praise that I have attracted. Indeed, now I do not even exult simply because of the love of my spouse and fine children (those wonderful people who sadly must someday die). Nor do I exult in the riches I have amassed in this life. No, now it is in YOU (O God) that I will rejoice and exult. (*Commentary on Psalm 9, 3*)

| PART TWO |

DEATH: THE DOOR TO LIFE

From the first moment that life begins every movement made hastens the approach of death. Every moment that is lived subtracts from the length of life and day after day less and less remains. Life now is nothing but a race toward death, a race in which no one can stand still or slow down even for a moment. All must run with equal speed and never-changing stride. For those who live a short time and those who live a long time, each day passes with unchanging pace. Both run with equal speed, one to a nearer, the other to a farther end. For both equally the lengthening minutes of passing life are left behind. Just as a long journey does not mean that travelers slow their steps, so on the way to death those who take more time, proceed no more slowly than those who seem to reach the goal more quickly. Indeed, all of us are in the process of dying from the moment of our birth. (*City of God*, 13.10)

Dying to Live

To the degree that anything is no longer what it was, and is now what it once was not, it is in the process of dying and beginning anew. (*Confessions,* 11.7.9)

—

At a philosophy meeting long ago I was "stuck" in a lecture hall listening to one of my confreres go on and on. His words were debilitating but his message was interesting. He said: "We have on earth not one life but a series of many lives. The life that goes before must die to give room to the life that is to follow." Sitting there, I proved his point. As he went on and on I slowly died, trapped in my seat. It took a good lunch to bring me back to life.

Thinking about the message later on, I began to appreciate the truth hidden in the language. Somehow or other we must die to where we are in the present moment if we are ever to make progress towards that next stage that is just around the corner. In a way life is a series of "deaths" as we move on to a new phase of our lives (*Commentary on Psalm 127,* 15). When we desperately try to hold onto our present moment, we in a way annihilate ourselves (reducing ourselves to a "nothing") because that "present" that we so desperately clutch at quickly slides away. Indeed, it does not seem to exist at all. In the words of Augustine: "If I look hard at the day which I clutch now, it does not seem to exist. My days do not have lasting 'being'; they depart almost before they arrive" (*Commentary on Psalm 38*, 7).

The reality of my life is that the present moment in which I try to define myself is flying by. If I define my "self" in terms of that elusive "present" and then look at myself from the perspective of the God who alone IS an eternal present, my substance is reduced to nothing at all (*Commentary on Psalm 38*, 9). The only definition of life that makes sense is a definition based on movement, the fact that I am constantly "dying" to the past so that I might "live" in the new moment that awaits me.

Now in my eighth decade I can see that this "dying" to one age so that we might "live" in the next is reflected in our desires and fears as we grow in age. We "lean into the future," looking forward to what is yet to be (*Letter 213*, 1). When we were little kids we longed to "grow up" so that others might take us seriously. We "played house" (if that was our inclination) or stood anxiously on the side-lines in the playground waiting to be "chosen" to join the teams playing the games that the big kids played, indifferent to being on one side or the other as long as we were chosen by somebody and thereafter treated like the "grown up" we so longed to be.

When we were adolescents (supposedly in the prime of our physical life), we worried that others would see our "gawkyness" as unattractive and would never come to know and love the exceptional "self" hidden deep inside our angular surfaces. We may have mocked the idea of dating or "going steady," but each morning we looked fearfully in the mirror for some new cataclysmic eruption that threatened our supposedly "perfect" complexion.

When we were in our twenties, we gloried in our physical strength and appearance but worried whether we would ever make a mark on the world, whether we would ever find someone who perhaps would love us deeply and forever. We began to search for the perfect job and perfect love that would make our lives worthwhile only to discover that the job of our dreams was far beyond our capacity and that the perfect love we had chosen for ourselves showed no interest in us.

When we were in our middle years, we worried that we had lost our opportunity to conquer the world. We longed for our days of youth as we tried to fend off the inevitable onset of age with its aches and pains. We began to look for something new to rejuvenate our sagging spirits (and body) only to find that the jogging and traveling and partying of our youth now only made us tired.

Finally, when we grew old, there was the pain of realizing that most of our life on earth was behind us. We wondered whether our lives had been all that worthwhile. We began to prepare for our final exit from the Hospice where we had lived out our earthly life.

Wisdom at any stage in our life is to realize that we must die to the past if we are to go on living that new life that is in front of us. Thus, when we fall in love, we must die to our solitary, uncaring days if we are ever to find that new wonderful life in the arms of our loved one. As we continue our life of love, sometimes at least we must "die" to the exuberant passion of our first feelings to begin to live in the deeper spiritual passion of a lifelong friendship. Finally, if our beloved leaves us in death, we must die to our life of companionship to begin alone a new life comforted only by memories. We still "care about" that great love of our life, but they are no longer present to be "lovingly cared for."

The wisdom of dying in order to live must also be part of every family's life. Eventually parents must die to loving their offspring as "children" in order to come to a new life of loving them as adults. Like it or not, the day comes when parents must "let go" of their offspring and allow them to make their own way in the world. They must die to being "nesting parents" to begin to live in a nest that is now empty. Their grown sons and daughters must also die as dependents in order to begin to live in the mature love of their parents as friends. Eventually, just as parents must move from "responsibility for" to "friendship with" their children as they grow older, so, too, children must die to the life of pleasant equality with parents to take up the chores of supporting them when they become disabled, dying to a life of simply "caring" about them to begin a life of "taking care of" them.

In terms of our earthly ambition, wisdom dictates that as we move on in life we must die to our old definition of success, putting aside those accomplishments that made us feel important when we were young (our first job delivering papers, playing childhood games well, graduating from school). If we do not die to the accomplishments of our growing up, we will never be prepared to live a creative active life in our mature years.

At last, when the time comes, we must be wise enough to allow our life of activity to pass away so that we can begin a new life of noble retirement. In truth, the transition is sometimes traumatic (especially if we have defined ourselves by our "doing") but there can also be a deep joy in this dying to the active life. Others no longer expect a lot from us. We no longer need to desperately paddle through life; we can just sit back and "go with the flow." It is especially pleasant if we are lucky enough to have a loved one who can and is willing to float along with us.

Augustine believed that we never lose the ages that are past; we just build on top of them. It is by this means that we can reach that full stature that the providence of God has determined should be ours. To refuse to move on in life is to prevent our growth, to condemn ourselves to a spiritual "dwarfism," refusing to be as big and tall as we were meant to be.

Furthermore, in desperately trying to go back, to hold onto the glories of past "lives" (as a "cute kid," as a "buff athlete," as a good-looking lover, as a "mover and shaker" on the world scene), we not only make fools of ourselves (there is nothing so absurd as a seventy-year-old adolescent), we also get in the way of those coming behind us. We do not have permanent residence here. Someday we must give up our rooms to others who follow: our kiddy room, our athlete's room, our "great lover" room, our "very important person" room. Augustine imagines the new-born child saying to its parents: "Well, I am here. Should you not be thinking about moving on, getting off the stage of life so that I can have the room to play my part?" (*Commentary on Psalm 127*, 15).

The consoling fact about our ever-moving life is that as we move through this Hospice we do not become homeless; we just move to larger rooms. Our faith assures us that the same thing will happen when we eventually die to this life itself. It will not be a movement to a dark "nowhere"; it will be a movement to an infinitely spacious room where we will be embraced by the arms of an infinite lover who will never let us go.

Dealing with Illness

People hope to be blessed by God in a variety of ways. Some wish for lasting health or a quick recovery if they fall sick. Who would deny that it is a great blessing not to be sick or to be cured swiftly when you become ill? (*Commentary on Psalm 66, #2*)

⟶

As we live out our days in this Hospice, this Inn for Travelers, it seems inevitable that sometimes we will not feel so good. No matter what we do, anxiety about getting sick and sadness when it comes are just part of our present condition. As the old Augustine somberly observed to the young Julian: "Everyone should face the fact that the misery which is a part of life extends from the tears of the newly born to the last breath of those soon to die" (*Incomplete Work Against Julian*, 1.50). In this life neither saint nor sinner can avoid pain. Indeed, the holier you are, the more you long for the peace that comes only when all illness is past and you are united forever with God (*City of God*, 20.17).

Although Augustine never seems to have experienced lasting good health (even as a child he almost died), he understood what being healthy meant. To be healthy means to have all your parts in good working order, to have the internal unity that is necessary for any "well-oiled" machine. Sickness, whether it be in the body or the spirit, is the absence of such unity, a time when the body begins to fall apart or when the spirit is torn by disturbing thoughts or disruptive desires. In sum, health is the condition of a well-ordered life that has a proper balance between a sound body and a healthy spirit (*City of God*, 19, 13, 1).

This peaceful unity is disrupted by ailments that infect the body and illusions that blight the soul (*Commentary on Psalm 37*, 5). The worst illusion is a reverse hypochondria whereby you are convinced that you are not sick when in fact you are. Augustine believed this to be the worst form of madness, a madness that makes any cure impossible: "In such cases a doctor can only be sorry for the one who rejects his help. He knows that the more convinced the patient is that he is not sick, the more dangerously ill he becomes" (*Sermon 80*, 3–4).

Second in seriousness to such mad denial is the person who accepts their spiritual weakness but believes that they can conquer it without the help of God (*City of God*, 22.23). They are swollen with a pride that makes it impossible to get through the "narrow gate" of heaven (*Sermon 142*, 5). Though in external appearance they may appear healthy, in fact they are on the verge of that "second death" that separates them from God forever (*City of God*, 12.1-2).

Our poor old bodies are perhaps the best antidote for such pride. Despite our pretense to be indestructible, no one can live very long without food, drink, and rest. We are always on the brink of death (*Commentary on Psalm 37*, 5), and it may come in unexpected ways. We can spend a lifetime avoiding dangerous situations only to be incapacitated by a small fever (*Sermon 19*, 6). The body (even when it is healthy) can become an unwilling servant of the spirit, badgering it with this or that temptation to indulge some illicit pleasure, saying to the spirit "I will not serve!" and thereby imitating the act of disobedience that caused the loss of paradise (*City of God*, 14.15.2).

Augustine believed that the corruption and sometimes illness of the body occurs because humans are now subject to death. If the first humans had obeyed God, they would have remained forever blessed and immortal in soul and body. That same divine doctor who now must come to cure the spiritually sick, in the beginning was rejected by humans who were still healthy and therefore eminently responsible for their bad decision (*Sermon 278*, 2). It is therefore incorrect to blame human misery on the impotence or injustice of God. The burden that humans now carry "from the day of their coming out of their mother's womb until the day they are buried in the earthy mother of all would not have existed had they not first rejected God" (*Against Julian*, 4.16.83). As things are now, the human nature that rejected the happiness of peace with God must suffer the misery of war with itself (*City of God*, 21.15). Such misery is only to be expected, and it is unjust to blame God for it. As Augustine observes: "It does not make sense to attribute blame when something is as it ought to be" (*Freedom of the Will*, 3, 15, 42).

It is indeed a shame that good people get sick and die, but their affliction may help them to know themselves more fully than they ever did before. Losing their health, they may become like the "free spirit" described in the book of Proverbs (11:25): "It does not stick fast in earthly things; its wings are not glued or entangled. Gleaming with splendid virtues it soars on the twin wings of two-fold love, freely into the upper air." And to this Augustine adds the consoling thought: "If you are good when you lose good things, God will be close at hand to comfort you" (*Commentary on Psalm 66*, 3).

Though it may be hard to realize it at the time, there is a goodness even in the pain humans feel when they lose a loved one. The pain is a sign of how deep and true was their affection. It can even have a therapeutic effect on the survivors if the agonizing fire of their loss reminds them of the transient nature of earthly things and moves them to look ahead to that life beyond death where all loves will be eternal (*On Eight Questions From Dulcitius*, 6; *On Faith and Works*, 28).

Sickness is always a lonely experience. When you are sick, it is not something that can be shared. We may look to others for sympathy, but they cannot know what we are going through. We are sick and (even if they themselves are not well) they do not have *our* sickness. When you are sick you do not look for sympathy so much as someone who will say to you, "I know what is wrong with you, and I know how to cure you." Their words do not cure us, but they do give us hope even when they do not know what to do for us right now.

Time passes slowly when you are sick. Waiting for a medicine that promises relief, we sometimes get impatient with our caregiver or with the God who seemingly is tardy in curing us. I suspect that Augustine was speaking from experience (perhaps as caregiver or invalid) when he wrote:

> Think what the demands of the sick are like. They think nothing so drawn out as the mixing of a drink for them when they are thirsty. The attendants are working fast to minimize the distress of the sick person yet he or she is demanding: "When is it coming? Isn't it cooked yet? When will they give it to me?" (*Commentary on Psalm 36/1*, #10)

For him such impatience of the sick is analogous to the impatience with God we sometimes feel when (apparently) he ignores us in our suffering.

In whatever form it takes, illness can change your view on life. Usually it is not too bad living in a pleasant Inn far from home as long as you feel good. You are having such a good time you may even forget that someday you need to go home. All that changes when you get sick. Even a minor illness can cause a change in careers. Dyspepsia at a philosopher's conference led to my eventual retirement. Increasing weakness in his lungs prompted the young Augustine to give up his position as speechmaker at the imperial court as "the pains in my chest made breathing difficult and my lungs would no longer support clear and prolonged speaking" (*Confessions*, 9, 2, 4). As an old man he experienced the disability that sometimes comes with an age that is "full of complaints, coughing, phlegm, bleary eyes, besieged with various aches and pains" (*Sermon 81*, 8). Such trials made him look forward to the day when he could finally end his stay in this Inn for weary travelers.

A minor illness may make you long for the land where illness does not exist; a serious illness sends the message that soon you will be exiting to such a land. Suddenly all that seemed so terribly important the day before your diagnosis becomes less so. You release your hold on your résumé outlining your past accomplishments, your degrees and awards. "What has been" becomes less significant than what is "now" and what "might be." You no longer strive to make people *look up to you;* now you want someone to care *about* you. If the past presses upon you, it is through regret for evil done and good undone. You look for someone with the power to tell you, "That's all right. Heaven is filled more with the penitent than with the guiltless." It is a consoling message, one that prompted Augustine in the last days of his long life to retire to his solitary room to happily sing the penitential psalms—that great song of those stained by an imperfect life.

One thing is certain: there is little we can do about spiritual unrest and bodily illness except to cope with them as best we can. Our pain when they are present and our anxiety in anticipating them will be eliminated only after death (*Sermon 53*, 3). All we can do now is to try to endure bravely the disabilities of life and pray that God will grant the grace to have the strength to follow the example of Christ and embrace with brave hearts the chalice of suffering if and when it comes (*City of God*, 22.22.4; *Sermon 88*, 6–7, 7).

Now in our days of health we should follow the advice of Augustine and imitate the ant "collecting seeds while it is still summer. During the barren days of your winter suffering you will then be able to eat what you have collected during those quickly passing fruit-filled days" (*Commentary on Psalm 66*, #3; cf. Prov 6:6-8).

When a Loved One Dies

As we live out our allotted time in this Hospice, we must come to realize that there will be different times for each of us to check out. Even at earthly gatherings it is rare that everyone leaves at the same time. At philosophy meetings, when I was scheduled to give the last talk of the day, it was not unusual to see some in the audience sitting there with bags packed and coats on, ready to exit at the first taste of boredom. In truth, I (even more bored and anxious to leave than they) wished that I could go with them but I could not. I still had my talk to finish and it was not yet my time to leave. And so it is now in the eighth decade of my life. Many of my friends and loves have already exited, but apparently I still have more words to say.

I was not too disturbed by those who left those academic conventions before me. I did not know them too well, and thus I did not miss them when they left. Such indifference is impossible when the one who leaves this Hospice without you is someone you love. Unfortunately it is in the nature of things that such parting happens more often than not. Either you exit before your loves (sad that you must leave them behind), or they depart before you, leaving you alone and anguished to face the rest of your life.

Augustine described this pain of loss to the people in his church:

> It is inevitable that we should be sad when those we love depart
> from us by dying. Although we know that they are not leaving

us forever, that they have but gone a little ahead of us, that we who remain will follow them, our nature still recoils from death. When death takes a loved one we are filled with sorrow simply because of our love for that person. In the death of those who are close to us we experience both sadness at the necessity of losing them and a hope that someday they will come back to us. Our human condition mourns their loss while our hope in the divine promises brings healing. (*Sermon 172*, 1)

To be honest, when I lose a loved one, my tears are very often just for myself. The great love of my life has gone, and now I am alone. My soulmate has gone, and now I have no one to talk to, no one with whom I can share my deepest feelings and thoughts, no one to whom I can reveal my heart and soul and fears and desires and imperfections. My beloved is gone, and I feel terribly alone even though I may be surrounded by a thousand others. They are only "others"; my love and I were an "us."

The death of a loved one must leave a gap in our lives if we truly loved them, and getting over the loss is never easy. Indeed, even having other loves does not ease the hurt. The fact that others whom we love are still with us does not take away the pain of the lost love who is with us no longer. To "get over" such a loss may seem almost impossible. If we truly loved our beloved, when they leave us in death they seem to take with them half our heart. We ask ourselves: "Would it not have been better never to have loved?" But then we realize that if we had never felt the ecstasy of love, the gap in our life would have been forever empty. We would literally have lived a *half-hearted* life.

This pain of loss is not taken away even when we believe that the loved one is still living someplace else. Even being a saint is no help. When he was a young man, Augustine lost a dear friend in death. Writing about it some twenty-five years later and now convinced of his friend's salvation, the pain of his loss is still evident. His description of how that death affected him spreads out through more than six chapters of his

Confessions. Some of what he said is contained in the following extended excerpts.

> My heart was darkened by sorrow and wherever I gazed I saw only death. Whatever I had shared with my dear friend became a source of agony without him. My town became a torture; my home, a house of unhappiness. I looked everywhere for him but to no avail. I hated every place that did not contain him. None of our old special spots would ever cry out again: "He is coming! He is coming!" as they did when he was alive but just absent for a while (*Confessions*, 4.4.9).
>
> I did not expect that my friend would return because of my tear-filled prayer. No indeed. The only reason why I wept was because he had been taken from me (*Confessions*, 4.5.10). Anyone who loves what must die is destined for such misery, a misery that comes not only when our loved one dies but even as we hold them in the last moments of their living (*Confessions*, 4.6.11).
>
> When I lost my friend, I was torn apart. I kept asking myself, "Why be sad?" But I had no answer that could take away my sadness (*Confessions*, 4.4.9). I could only weep. And yet, I still preferred my own tacky life to ending our separation by joining him in death. I hated my lonely life but was afraid to die. The more I loved him, the more I feared the death that had snatched him away, the death that would eventually consume all humans as it had consumed him. I wondered how other mortals could continue living when this one I had loved so deeply was now dead. I wondered even more how this dear friend who was part of me could die and yet I continue to live. Indeed Horace spoke the truth when he called his friend "half my soul" (*Carmina*, 1.3.8). I felt as though my friend's spirit and mine had really been but one spirit housed in two bodies. My life was unbearable because it had been cut in half by his death. And yet, I feared to die, lest that last part of my friend (the love I still cherished in my heart) should perish and he would become completely dead (*Confessions*, 4.6.11).
>
> When my friend died, I raged and wept and became confused. I could not think straight. I was immune to good advice. There was no rest. I carried about a cut and bleeding spirit that

was reluctant to be anywhere. I could find no place to put it to rest. It could not be consoled by pleasant walks in the forest nor could it be distracted by games or songs or aromatic gardens or fine meals or the pleasures of the bed. It could not concentrate on books or be at rest in poems. All things, even light itself became unbearable and loathsome. Only my weeping and moaning seemed easy. When I tried to stop my anguish I became even more sorrowful (*Confessions*, 4.7.12).

I was a place of sorrow, a place I could not bear to be but from which I was too weak to flee. Where after all could my heart escape from my heart? Where could I hide from myself? How could I elude a pursuer who turned out to be me? I told myself "Hope in God!" But I could not. My friend who had been lost was more real to me than the vague image of God I was supposed to hope in (*Confessions*, 4.4.9).

I knew that in some way I had to lift my spirit to you, O Lord. But I could not do it. Indeed, I could not do it because you seemed too vague and unsubstantial to my way of thinking. I thought that you were just a fantasy. Indeed, my error was my God. If I had tried to rest my spirit on such a fragile deity, it would only have fallen through the void and plummeted empty back to me (*Confessions*, 4.7.12). O God, if you were everywhere, why were you not there when I was in agony! Were you just too busy with other things when I was being torn apart? (*Confessions*, 4.5.10).

There is no question that Augustine's grief consumed his young life. It was like a raging fire that destroyed everything thrown into it: good advice, comforting words, new experiences, prayers, even God. Eventually he was able to recover and get on with his life. But, as the following passages indicate, it was not easy:

The consolation of friends did the most to repair the damage and give me strength after the death of my loved one. The things between us captured my mind: conversations and joking, doing favors for each other, reading good books together, being foolish and being serious together, disagreeing without hatred almost as though one were disagreeing with oneself, sometimes falling into conflict but realizing thereby in how many things we agreed, teaching and learning from each other, waiting impatiently for absent friends to return and rejoicing when they did. These and similar signs coming from the hearts of friends and loved ones are manifested through the eyes and the mouth and speech and a thousand gestures. They bring together hearts like bundled kindling, making one from many (*Confessions*, 4.8.13).

Time has passed, Lord, and the wound has softened (*Confessions*, 4.5.10). Time never stays long in one place. It never idles in passing through our lives and its flowing motion does wonders for our minds. After the death of my friend, days came and went and in their coming and going they eventually introduced memories of events other than those of my dead friend. The passing of time slowly brought hopes other than those that had been based on my loved one's presence. Little by little I was reintroduced to my former pleasures and my pain of loss began to fade away (*Confessions*, 4.8.13). Eventually, however, I just had to get out of that town, thinking that my eyes would look less for my dead friend in a place where I was unaccustomed to seeing him alive (*Confessions*, 4.7.12).

Later on, Augustine tried to understand why his grief had been so deep. He concluded that it was the result of two facts about human nature. The first is very good: we are beings who are meant to love. The second is not so good: because we are "cracked" we sometimes tend to love wildly. Now more or less recovered from his grief, Augustine asked himself:

Why had I been so easily overcome with sorrow? Was it not because I had poured out my soul on shifting sand by loving one who was sure to die as though he would never die? (*Confessions*, 4.8.13). How crazy it is, not knowing how to love a human being like a human being! How foolish to be so uncontrolled in clutching a loved one! And yet that is how I was when my friend died (*Confessions*, 4.7.12).

Such is the passion we have for those we love that we feel guilty if love is not given to them even when there is no response beyond some modest signs of their good will. This passionate love is the source of the grief we feel when a loved one dies. This is the reason for the agony that clouds our life, the tears that bathe our hearts, our dying from sorrow while we are still alive (*Confessions*, 4.9.14).

Loving so intensely is a human tendency, and perhaps it is better than its opposite: not loving at all. But it can lead to crushing agony when the loved one departs. To avoid this, we can only try to keep in mind the true nature of existence this side of death, that it is a passing parade in which each one dances for a while and then moves on, leaving the stage to other players who come after. Our loved ones come and go and all we can do is try to love them in the right way, loving them in the way described by Augustine in his final reflection:

> Happy the man, O Lord, who loves you and loves his friend in you and loves his enemy because of you. For no one ever loses a loved one forever who cherishes them in and through that one who is never lost, that one who is our God (*Confessions*, 4.9.14).

Augustine's experience shows that even the greatest sorrow can be cured by the passage of time. But to be cured the grieving person must get on with life, filling up the empty places of the past with new prospects for the future. As in Augustine's case, sometimes a change of place is required. Memories can be precious or painful but if they are unremittingly painful, it is best to do away with the places that cause them.

To fill up life with new life is best accomplished through other friends and other loves. We need hospice care at every moment of our lives but especially when we are in the depths of grief over the loss of one we loved. Others must lift us up by being with us and developing with us new experiences, new joys, new passions. When I was little, wading through the shallows at the seashore, I would sometimes fall into a hole left by a departed friend's excavation in the sand. The hole was deep and seemed always to be there, twisting me in knots whenever

I fell into it. I eventually learned that the only way I could avoid the pain was to float above it on the new incoming tide. Later I thought to myself that this is the way we survive the loss of someone we loved deeply. The hole in our heart left by their passing never disappears but somehow we are able to rise above it, carried by the incoming tide of love from friends who rush in to support us. We never forget the one who at one time filled that gap in our lives but we are no longer crippled by their absence. Nostalgia gradually takes over, that sweet gentle word for remembered good times that can never return. Through such fond memories our grief may finally begin to be softened.

Dealing with Death

We think of the dead when we carry them out to be buried. We say: "Poor fellow, only yesterday he was walking around!" (or) "I saw him less than a week ago and he spoke to me of this and that. But now he is no more."

This is what we say. But we think this way only as long as we are weeping for the dead and busy about the funeral. We bury the thought of death along with our dead friend. We put aside the thought that someday it will be our turn to die. Instead we return to our life of fraud, stealing, perjury, drunkenness, and the endless pleasures of the flesh. (*Sermon 361,* 5)

I hope it does not seem too morbid to talk about death in the midst of life. It just makes sense to me as long as I am in this Inn for Travelers to consider every once in a while that I will not be here forever, that some day (perhaps a day not of my choosing) I must check out. It may not be pleasing, but that's the way it is.

I admit that there is a reluctance to think about leaving when you are having a good time. When you are on vacation and are enjoying yourself, leaving is your last concern. Perhaps you have found friends who seem to care for you and who help make your days more pleasant. Perhaps you have found one whom you dearly love but who must be left behind when you go. Even though you may know that you are going home, you don't think about it when you are in the arms of your beloved.

Indeed, leaving can be frightening if you are not quite sure where you are going. It's all well and good to return to a comfortable place where you have been before, but to go to a new place, an unknown place, can bring a high level of anxiety. On my first (and only) trip to Rome, I knew I was going to a place where I had never been before and various questions plagued me:

How will they understand me?

Will they lose my bags with all my precious possessions?

Will the people there like me?

Will they treat me as an alien easily dismissed?

Where will I find rest in such a strange city?

Of course in earthly travel a lot of these anxieties can be solved by listening to those who have been there before, by making reservations, by taking out insurance. But how can this be done when the mysterious place I am going is to the other side of death?

Sometimes we cry out: "WHY OH WHY IS IT *ME* THAT MUST DIE!" and the answer that comes back is that all of us are made up of parts that are falling apart. Our body parts are in constant flux. Every seven years we have a mostly new body, which in our early years was better than what was left behind but which later on begins to show signs of inevitable decay. Christian theology tells us that our death is nothing more than our body literally "giving up the ghost," separating from that spirit that held it together and gave it life (*City of God*, 13.2).

The phrase used on Ash Wednesday is inaccurate in this regard. To say "Remember man, that you are dust and unto dust you shall return" ignores the fact that the human being is more than the body. However, it is instructive in that when the body "turns to dust" the "I" that is the whole person no longer exists. We seem to recognize this truth whenever we go to a wake for a dead friend. Entering the front door we ask "Where is his *body*?" not "Where is HE?" Though we may believe in the immortality of his soul, we sense that the question "Where is HE?" has no answer just then.

This is the source of much of the dismay we feel when faced with the fact of death. Death may be the door to life, but as long as our spirit is separated from our now dissolved body the life we have is at best incomplete. Perhaps that is the reason why Augustine preferred to describe our life after death and before resurrection as a kind of sleep (*Sermon 172*, 1). When we sleep we have something like a disembodied existence. If we are lucky (and as you age you sometimes are not that lucky), you rest peacefully unconscious of the presence of your body. Your life is still conscious, but it is a dream life populated by pleasures and pains, friends and enemies, loves and acquaintances who exist now only in your dreams. Though it may be peaceful, it is not the ideal state for your living spirit. Your spirit has a natural desire to be united with the body, to wake up and find its old friend still attached (*A Literal Commentary on Genesis*, 7.27.38).

Indeed the perfection of our happiness depends not on our spirit's flight from the corruptible body but on its eventual union with an incorruptible body (*City of God*, 13.20). No one hates their own body. They only hate the fact "that it is mortal, that it is wasting away, that it is corroding" (*Sermon 242a*, 3). We don't want to escape the body; we want to have an incorruptible body. The body is good in itself. If corruption were taken away from the body, spirit and body would be friends forever (*Sermon 155*, 14.15). The glory of resurrection is that once again the two friends, body and soul, will get together. Then we will truly be in heaven. The time of separation in the interim between life and LIFE is more like a purgatory, not too bad but certainly not as good as it could be.

Nothing can be done about the fact that we will someday die. Augustine uses the analogy of an oil lamp to make this point. A lamp is filled with light only because it is constantly burning off its resource of oil. If it burns a long time, the light begins to flicker and die as its source of energy is used up. The light can be kept burning only by supplying new oil. However, the time will come for all lamps when the light dies forever because the wick deteriorates. Even at its brightest moments this essential element of the lamp is slowly being eaten away by time and by use (*Sermon 362*, 11).

We humans are like living lamps. We must take nourishment over a lifetime in order to maintain our vital activities. It might seem to the simple that as long as we have enough to eat and drink our life can go on forever. But this cannot happen. Our "wick" is slowly wasting away. The very vessel in which the vital activity is carried on is itself corroding, wearing down, and wearing away. The day will come when it can no longer support the flame of life no matter how much nutriment is poured into it. When that day comes, the body falls apart, the soul escapes, and the human dies.

This is the common lot of every human being, and nothing can be done to prevent it from eventually happening to each one of us (*City of God*, 1.11). The day will come when we must check out of this Hospice, leaving all our loves and things behind, carrying with us only the memory of delightful days. As Augustine told his church congregation:

> To be born and to die, the beginning and the end: these are the two facts of our lives. By being born we begin our labors, by dying we move on to an uncertain future. These two facts we know. They are the constant facts we must face in this our land. (*Sermon 229E*, 1)

Understandably, most of us try not to face this fact as long as we can. After all, when you are at a party, it is hard to leave. Two friends of mine left their wedding reception with much joy, only to return an hour later. A short distance down the road they decided that there was more certain fun at the reception they had left than in unknown life ahead. So, too, when we face the prospect of leaving this life, we sometimes try to put off our leaving as long as possible, paying great sums of energy and capital as a price for a few more days in this Inn. But the effort is of little use. It is like a little child sticking its hand out the window of a speeding car, trying to slow its progress towards the hated school.

The fact of the matter is that we all move towards death at a constant speed. To use Augustine's phrase, we are all "in death" as soon as we are conceived (*City of God*, 13.10), and our increasing day by day feebleness is but the extension of our future death into our present moment (*Commentary on Psalm 84*, 10). Human history is nothing more than the continuing story of the dying giving up their places to the newly born (*City of God*, 15.1).

Since our future death is inevitable, it makes sense to deal with it now, to recognize the fact that this life is not forever and to make plans accordingly (*Letter 10*, 2). Sometimes we do not do this. We try to ignore our death by living life more frantically, hiding from the future by our busy involvement in the present (*Letter 10*, 2). Such compulsive concentration on the present does not make sense. The human is a being of past, present, and future, and all times must be kept in mind if we are to be truly wise. Recognizing our limited future in this life, we can come to a more reasonable love for the things we have and the friends we cherish, enjoying them here and now but realizing that they will not be forever. Recognition of the fact of death can make us more detached from perishable things and allow us to face our end in greater freedom and (perhaps) with lessened fear (*Letter 10*, 2).

Certainly the fact that we shall someday die should not make us forget that we are alive right now. We still have some time here and now to enjoy truth, love, and the other goods that are part of this passing life. The present moment is terribly important for each of us. It is at this present moment that we can work to insure that our future will be happy, both our life after death and our death itself. As Augustine consoled his friends who were worrying about death: "Anyone who lives a good life is not able to have a bad death" (*Sermon 249*, 2).

Fearing Death

Those who do not fear death should examine themselves closely lest perhaps they are in fact already dead. (*Sermon 348*, 3)

—

Even if I have been able to deal with my death by facing up to its inevitability, this does not mean that I will no longer fear its coming. Despite my present aches and pains, I still do not want to die. Does this indicate some weakness in me, some lack of faith? Augustine's answer is a resounding "NO!" As he told the people in his church: "Death is not able to be loved, only tolerated. By nature not only humans but indeed every living thing abhors death and fears it" (*Sermon 299*, 8). What he was saying is that the reason why I don't want to die is not because I am a coward, but because I am a human being with a thirst for unending life.

Now in my dotage, I am still like that little kid I once was, fighting to stay awake on Christmas Eve. I fought sleep because I was enjoying the place and time where I was. My family was busy about putting up the Christmas tree. Happy music was playing, and every once in a while I was able to steal a candy cane. But then I was told to go upstairs and go to sleep, to lose awareness of all the good and happy things that were happening in my house. Of course, I was promised that if I went to sleep

I would wake up to a wonderful new day, a day in which (though I had missed seeing Santa) I would experience the wonder at what he had left behind. My condition would be something like that of Moses seeing only the "back part of God" as he quickly passed by (Exod 33:21-23).

The promises of what I would see when I rose from sleep were truly fantastic but I feared that they might be nothing more than fantasy. The grand noises and smells and songs and sights of Christmas Eve were the only *reality* I could comprehend. I had never consciously experienced Christmas morning before. For me it existed only in the stories of those who had gone before me. And so it is now facing my sleep of death. As it was in my baby days, the time will come when I will be forced to sleep, but I will fight against that final drowsiness as long as I can.

My reluctance to die is understandable. I know what I have and most of the time I have come to enjoy it. It is natural to fear change when I am in the midst of a life that is flourishing, a life that has not as yet gone sour, an interesting life without too much pain, an exciting life with some loves to surround me in good times and rally around when the times go bad. When the good quality of life here at this Inn disappears, I may be quite ready to check out, but just now I am comfortable where I am, and I fear losing what I have come to love.

The trouble with dying is like facing my first Christmas Day. I don't know exactly what the promised "new day" will be like. A "life after life" is a place I have never been before. I am told that when I leave this Hospice, I will go to a land where the sun is always shining and the air is always fresh, but I have never seen this wonderful place. Where I am now, it may rain from time to time, the air-conditioning may not always work, the air is sometimes polluted by passing traffic, but at least I am dealing with something I know. The promised magic world beyond the door of this Hospice is an unknown, and it is natural for me to fear the unknown despite the promises of those who claim to have been there.

I know and like where I am; where I am going is still a mystery. However, one thing IS certain: when I get there I will be changed radically. When I was little, I was not afraid that I would disappear when I went to sleep. Perhaps this was because I got used to peaceful sleeping in my mother's womb. Waking up after birth was the new experience and I cried out in fright. I was not used to that new land of bright lights and robed giants. When I sleep in death there will be an even more dramatic change. I will no longer be "ME." If I am "me" through the union of my body and soul, then death at very least must cause a diminution of my "ME-NESS," a lessening that will cause a new sort of existence that I cannot understand and therefore cannot love. I will be "wrenched apart" and I fear the consequences.

Augustine suggests that this natural antipathy towards death was present in the first humans even before they knew of the possibility. Neither Adam nor Satan belittled death. It is true that Adam was threatened with death if he disobeyed God. It is also true that he sinned anyway, but this was not because he did not fear death. He simply did not believe that it applied to him (*Sermon 335B*, 1).

Augustine believed that even though the Christian martyrs chose death, they did not cease to love this life. They simply loved the next life more. Their faith convinced them that they would live through their death, and their fortitude gave them the strength to get through it. But it is only with the help of the grace of God that they were able to develop such faith and fortitude (*Sermon 335b*, 4). He adds that the great apostle Peter himself was not exempt from this fear of death. Augustine sees this fear implied in Christ's words to him: "When you grow old, another will bind you and bear you where you do not wish to go" (John 21:18). Christ was speaking about Peter's eventual martyrdom but the now elderly Augustine saw the words as applicable to all who suffer the lessened powers of old age, observing sadly: "and so it goes when you grow old" (*Sermon 335b*, 3). His point is that we are carried to our deaths whether on the cross or in our beds by forces that we have no control over. We must die and we are not in favor of it at all.

Augustine suggests that even Jesus-God was not happy about the prospect of his own death. Of course, he chose to die, but this does not mean that he enjoyed it. On the contrary, he asked that the chalice of his suffering be taken away, and it was not. Jesus went through his death reluctantly so that he might show us that he understands our fear when we come to face our own death. Augustine adds that the reason why Jesus wept at the tomb of Lazarus was not because his friend had died (since he knew he would presently bring him back to life) but rather because of the sad fact of death itself. Augustine asks:

> Why would he weep over a dead man that he was about to bring back from the grave by a simple command? The explanation is that he did not weep for the dead Lazarus whom he was to raise up. He wept about death itself, that death that humans brought upon themselves by their sins. (*Sermon 173, 2*)

Over the years I have been encouraged by those whom I have seen in their last days who seemed to simply "sleep their way into eternity." Mostly free of pain (thanks to a kind and understanding medical staff), they died free of anxiety, surrounded by some who cared for them. Their passage was quiet and without fear. True, some were unconscious, but what's wrong with that? I have always been mystified by the doctors who told my suffering friend Marion: "There is nothing we can do for your pain because you are not terminal!" Not terminal? We are all and always will be terminal at every moment of life and anything anyone can do to cure our pain or at least be with us in our pain is performing a great act of kindness.

It seems that this kindness was shown to Augustine at the end. Despite the fear of death that he carried throughout his life, he exited this Hospice peacefully. As Possidius, his biographer and friend, describes it:

During his last days he was given the quiet to pray. Finally, with all the members of his body intact, his sight and hearing unimpaired and while we looked on and prayed at his bedside, he "slept with his fathers, well-nourished in a good old age." (Possidius, *Life of St. Augustine*, 31)

The encouraging message from Augustine's death is that if we have tried to live with love for others and love for God, at the end of life we will have the divine support to die without fear. And, if we are *really* lucky, we will be surrounded by some who loved us and stood by us as we lived out our days in this Hospice, this Inn for Travelers.

Images of Death:
"Piercing the Dome"

What can be said about our future? The prospect prompted Paul to cry "The dark times of this life cannot be compared to the future glory that shall be revealed to us" (Rom 8:18). What in the world can this glory be? Nothing else than to truly SEE! . . . to be like the angels and see the light that is God. What a great gift is given to a blind man when the doctor comes and cures his blindness! To finally see the LIGHT! The cured blind man may give his healer gold piled upon gold, but his healer gave HIM light! What then shall we give to divine physician who heals the eyes of our spirit so that we can come to see the eternal light? (*Commentary on Psalm 36/2, 8*)

For some years now (perhaps because I am in my eighth decade), I have been wondering more and more about what the *process of dying* is like. I am not speaking here about what *being dead* is like, what it is like when my soul departs from this body, what it will be like when it is reunited to my body at resurrection. I believe (by the grace of God and the promise of Jesus Christ) that there *is* life after death and that there will be *resurrection* eventually, and I hope to reflect on these issues in another place, but right now I wish to consider only the *process* of getting beyond the grave, to ask: "What will *dying* be like?"

Of course, I have no certain knowledge about this process any more than I had certain knowledge of what falling in love would be like before I experienced it (many times, as things turned out). Before it actually happens, I can only *imagine* what my dying will be like, and one image that has been recurring most powerfully is that my dying will be like *piercing the dome*.

This image of dying was suggested to me by my former reading of Greek philosophy and by a recent popular movie. The movie was *The Truman Show,* and it told the story of a man who lived out his whole life in a huge dome created by a T.V. network. His life was much like the lives of any of us as we live out our time on earth. He did not know until the very end that he (like us?) was living in a dome, a confined fantasy world, and that there was a great unknown world (the real world) outside.

At the end of the movie, Truman discovered the truth about his life. He finally found the door leading outside the dome and, looking up at the hidden cameras, he said his farewell to the watching audience: "Till I see you again, my friends, I can only say 'Good night! Good morning! Good afternoon.'"

Then he bowed, turned around, and went through the door to the unknown darkness accompanied by the cheers of the T.V. audience who witnessed his exit. I sometimes think that (if I had the courage) those would be great words to say as I passed beyond the dome of this life to the unknown eternity outside, perhaps to the cheers of those witnesses (human, angelic, divine) in eternity who had all the while been watching my laborious progress through my somewhat "make-believe" life here in time.

This image of "piercing the dome" was also suggested to me by the description of this world given by Plato. He pictured our life now as being in a cave where at best all we can see are shadows of the "real world" outside. If we live a noble life here within the confines of our domed cave, someday we will be worthy to "pierce the dome," exit the cave, and see what is *truly real* in all its brilliance.

In ancient Greece many believed that when we look to the sky on a clear night, we get a hint of that wonderful land of the gods in the specks of light that we see. The stars and the moon are nothing more than "cracks" in the dark dome that encases our life now, cracks that allow the fiery brilliance of the land beyond to shine through.

Though many of those ancient thinkers (Plato was an exception) had no clear idea of personal immortality, of being able to someday pierce that dome themselves and enter the kingdom of light, their glimpse of that land "beyond the dome" gave them an understanding of what their own world was really like: an imperfect clouded world that would not be forever. Many did not necessarily consider the world of fire beyond the dark dome of the sky as being a *better* world than this, nor did many of them see any way of continuing to exist if somehow or other they could exit this present dome to that bright world of fire outside. In this they differed from Truman. He was able to escape his "domed life" and move to join all those folks who had watched him and loved him as he made his way through his days in the "unreal" world inside the dome.

For Truman and for those ancient civilizations who believed it possible, there was an understandable fear of entering that great unknown world beyond the walls of their accustomed life. The "great beyond" was for them, as it is for us, a frightening prospect.

Although Augustine does not use the image of "piercing the dome" to explain the process of dying, he would agree that the life we lead now is in a sense like living in a confined fantasy world. Indeed, he goes even further. He contends that when this life is compared to the life we can have in heaven, this life does not even seem to exist, that when we compare our personal reality now (our *being*) with the infinite reality that is God, we seem to become almost *non-being*, nothing at all. He asks:

> Does that day in which you *are* now not exist? Well, I have to say that if I look hard, it does not exist. If I compare the passing

things of this life with those eternal things that abide forever, I can clearly see what has *true being* and what has more the *appearance of being*. Am I to say that these present days of mine have *true being*? Shall I be so rash as to use the great word "BEING" of this flux of things that slide toward extinction? For myself, in my weakness, I am so nearly *non-existent* that I cannot even understand the God who said: "I AM WHO AM"! (*Commentary in Psalm 38, 7*)

Of course (as Augustine admits), our present life has some substance to it if only the "soap-opera" reality of Truman's fantasy life inside the dome. But faith tells us that someday we will pass through that door of death, we will "pierce the dome" and arrive at the land of the God who truly *is*. If we have been faithful in this life, we will finally be able to see the brilliance of that land of light in which there is no past or future, no "coming and going," only an eternal "now" in the presence of the infinite God.

Sadly there is another terrifying possibility. Whether we have been vicious or virtuous in this life, someday we shall certainly die, but if our life has been a life of unrepentant evil, turning our back on God in time, then our eternity will be spent separated from him who is INFINITE BEING. If that is our terrible fate (and it will be so only if we choose to make it so), then it can truly be said that our fate beyond the dome will be, not *to be*, but *to be nothing at all*.

Through faith we have been given some information about that world beyond the dome, that world beyond the doors of this Hospice. We can see that (like Truman and the denizens of Plato's cave) we, too, are faced with the challenge of "going beyond the confining walls of our accustomed life" with the hope that something truly good awaits us, a world not of darkness but of shining light where we can at last see all those who have known us and loved us. Our faith also tells us that we are on the edge of eternity at every moment of our lives. Even now, if we could reach out far enough with our spirit, we would feel the smooth surface of the thin wall that separates our present confined life from the brilliant boundless eternity that awaits us once we have "pierced the dome" separating life from life.

Images of Death:
"To Sleep, Perhaps to Dream"

After all, what else is sleep but a daily death, a sleep which does not definitively remove us from here and now, a sleep that does not last all that long? And what else is death but a long-lasting and very deep sleep, a sleep from which God will wake us up one day. (*Sermon 221*, 3)

⟶

The question "What is death like?" is as difficult to answer as the previous question "What is dying like?" It asks for a description of our state at the moment after our "dying" is done. Just as we have yet to experience the "moment of death" (what we have called "the piercing of the dome") so, too, we have no personal experience of the "moment after death." Others may have told us about their "near death" experience, but even if they had such an experience, it would still be their experience and not ours.

Accepting the testimony of others about important facts of life (like loving or giving birth or being sick) is always difficult. We tend to accept their words with a "grain of salt," believing that they are making too much (or too little) of the experience. Faith is never easy because it depends on the testimony of others and is often less convincing than having the experience ourselves. We do not really know what love is until we ourselves feel it. Others may write about it and sing about it, but love is an experience that cannot be truly appreciated until we have it for ourselves. The same is true of pain or depression or dying. Other kind souls may come up to us and sympathize and say, "I know just how you feel," but they cannot because they are not the ones in pain or depressed or dying.

One author has suggested that mystics like St. Teresa of Avila came not only to "not-fear" death but even to love it because they had momentarily experienced it, both the brief wrenching pain of the separation of body and soul and the subsequent ecstasy of "seeing of God." But even if this were true, their experience is still theirs and not ours, and presumably before they had the perception of "being dead" they were just as disturbed by the prospect as the rest of us.

An attempt to imagine what death will be like will, of course, be different for those who believe in personal immortality and those who do not. Both groups would at least agree that when you are dead the body ceases its activity and eventually disintegrates. For those who do not believe in the existence and immortality of the soul, a "spirit" that continues on after the process of dying is over, death can only mean oblivion and nothing more.

Those who believe that death is the end of all life face a great difficulty in trying to describe what such a "death-state" is like. I exist and I know what that means, but how can I describe "non-existence" beyond saying that my death means that I no longer exist? It is simply oblivion. For those of us who have gotten used to "being something," the prospect of "being nothing" can be the most terrifying prospect of life. Augustine, who so relished being alive, was frankly amazed at those who seemed to be unafraid of death even though convinced that there was nothing more. He confessed that he could never be happy facing such final personal extinction (*Soliloquies*, 2.23).

When he eventually came to believe in his personal immortality (and it took him thirty years to become convinced), he began to wonder what such "life after death" might be like. It was evident to him that a person's experience immediately after death did not involve the body because the body decomposes at death. The awareness in death must then be a perception of a soul or spirit now separated from its body. But what in the world could such an experience by a disembodied soul be like? In this life our experience is centered around the body, its pleasures and pains, its growth and decline. It takes great attention and even greater virtue to experience our spirit.

Augustine accepted the existence of his spiritual soul, but the nature of its life after death remained a mystery. Would it be conscious? Would it know what was going on in the lives of those left behind? Would it be able to visit with them in some way? Would it be able to do anything for them, give them consolation, help them in their need?

In trying to answer such questions, he depended on Scripture and his own experience to come up with a description that was both reasonable and comforting. For him the explanation that best met these criteria was that "being dead" was something like "being asleep." However, he recognized that although all the dead will be in a place of rest, all will not rest peacefully. Only those who are saved will anticipate the joys of heaven (perhaps dulled a bit by the scars of their previous virtuous but imperfect lives). Those who have earned condemnation will begin to feel the pain of the full-blown hell that awaited them after resurrection (*Enchiridion: Faith, Hope, and Charity*, 29.109). The sleep of death will not be an unconscious state. Immediately after death the spirit will be aware of its fate and will begin to taste the full joy or despair that will come with resurrection (cf. *Sermon 223C*).

Scripture itself seems to support this contention of conscious life and activity after death. We are told that Christ's body slept in his tomb on Holy Saturday, but at the same time his spirit descended to the place of the dead. As Peter wrote in his first letter: "He was put to death insofar as fleshly existence goes, but was given life in the realm of the spirit. It was in the spirit also that he went to preach to the spirits in prison" (1 Pet 3:18-19). An ancient sermon given on Holy Saturday expands on Peter's message:

> There is a great silence on earth today, a great silence and still-ness. The whole earth keeps silence because the King is asleep. The earth trembled and is still because God has fallen asleep in the flesh and he has raised up all who have slept ever since the world began. . . . Greatly desiring to visit those who live in darkness and in the shadow of death, he has gone to free from sorrow the captives Adam and Eve, he who is both God and the son of Eve. He took them by the hand and raised them up say-ing: "Awake, O sleepers, and rise from the dead and I, the Christ, will give you light." (*Second Reading from Office of Readings: Holy Saturday* PG 43, 439.451.462–63)

Augustine did not believe that the dead were directly aware of what is going on here on earth. However, he leaves open the possibility that events might be revealed to them either by God or by those who had more recently died. He reasoned that if the dead are in a place of rest it would seem that they would be preserved from the suffering that comes from seeing their still living loved ones live out their somewhat painful lives.

As far as the dead being able to return from the grave with important messages for the living, Augustine believed that it was not in their power to do so (though God could allow it for good reasons). He was convinced that if the dead could do it on their own, nothing would have stopped his mother Monica from giving sage advice to him whenever he fell asleep. She never let him alone when she was alive; given the chance, she would never have left him alone when she was dead.

The conclusion of all this speculation (and that is all it is) is that when we are dead and on the way to join the Blessed in heaven, we may still remember the past but our consciousness will be more focused on our present condition (that we have "MADE IT"!) and on the glorious future that awaits us after resurrection (*Care of the Dead*, 15.18–16.19; 13.16).

There is still the puzzle of how we, during this interim period between dying and being resurrected, can be asleep and yet be aware of our condition. Perhaps the answer is suggested by the dreaming sleep that we frequently experience in this life. In such dreams we have a consciousness that seems to be independent of what is happening to our body at the moment. In our dreams we can revisit the past and imagine the future. We combine and recombine images that never were and never will be, sometimes revisiting old loves that once were, sometimes embracing those we had loved and still love but who were never aware of our affection or (worse still) rejected it.

Sometimes the dreams are steeds that carry us to pleasant places, and we wish they would go on forever. At other times they are the mares of night that ride through our sleeping consciousness, leaving terror in their wake. In this life we are saddened or relieved when our good or bad dreams end, but after death the dreams will not end, constantly aggravating or pleasing us until the day of resurrection when they will blend naturally into the horrific or ecstatic eternity that awaits us. For some the wait to be awakened will be long; for others it will be quite short. But for everyone the waking will be forever (*Commentary on the Gospel of John*, 49.10).

For Augustine the question of what being dead was like was not all that important. When we die we will know and before we die we can only guess. But this we do know: if we have done our best in life to be faithful and have been sorry when we have inevitably failed, then God will take care of our eternal future. Sleeping or awake we shall be very, very happy. We shall "depart to an ecstasy which knows no fear and has no end" (*Sermon 399*, 13).

Helping the Dying

We need hospice care at every moment of our lives. This is so because we are in a "strange" place no matter how long we live here and how much we get used to it. At one time this Hospice, this Inn for Travelers, did not exist; at some future time it will not exist again. This is the reason why, in our search for happiness, we always could use a little help from our friends. This is especially true at the last moments of life when finally we must face our imminent death.

Over the years I have been called upon from time to time to act as a chaplain for the dying, spending time "being with" those who were at the end of life and afterward with those who grieved over the death of their loved one. I say "being with" advisedly because long ago I discovered that there are no pat, pious phrases, no forms of speech, that will guarantee consolation to the dying or to those who love them.

I remember standing outside the hospital room of a young mother who was soon to die, wondering what in the world I could say to her about death that would help her face it. I found that I did not need to say anything. She, with the help of God, was already accepting her death with equanimity. I was company for her more than a problem solver, and that seemed to be quite enough at the time. My clerical collar helped only in that it was a sign that I might be one who would not be embarrassed being in the presence of the dying.

It is not easy for any of us "to help others to die." We want to make them happy, but death seems to contradict everything we need to be happy: life, meaning, and love. It is true that sometimes we look forward to death as a blessing, but this is not because we don't want to live. Rather, it is because we hope (if we are a believer) to enter a better life or (if we are not a believer) because oblivion seems preferable to the diminished life that illness imposes on us. I think this is what happened to a friend of mine who put a gun to his head and shot himself the day after the doctors told him he had cancer. He wanted to live but he did not want to impose on himself nor on his family the few months of the "half-life" that the doctors had promised him.

It is hard for the dying to find meaning in their lives when they become completely dependent on others. We humans tend to measure our importance by our ability to control our present and provide for our future. It is difficult to feel you are worth something when you cannot even take care of your most basic bodily functions, depending on others to be fed, to be cleansed, to move about. In this regard, I think of a man I knew who at one time was very active in carrying God's message to the world. He traveled freely over the earth and people listened and wondered at his power. When he became old and paralyzed, he cried out in the middle of the night when he could not find the remote control for the T.V. That small device became important to him in his last days because it was the only instrument of autonomy left to him. Through it he could turn off and on pictures of a world that he would never travel again. Old and paralyzed, he could not change his life, but at least he could still change the channels.

We cannot give the dying their life back nor the things that made them important in the eyes of the world, but we can still fulfill their desire to be loved. We begin doing that by *accepting them as they are*. In dealing with those who are coming to the end of their days in this Hospice, it is terribly important to accept them as we find them and be sensitive to what they "want" rather than what we "think" they "need." We may have a passion to talk about death in general and their death in particular, but the dying person may not wish to know that they are dying or at least may not wish to talk about it. If they need to fantasize about being cured, it is Christian charity to run with that fantasy about living while at the same time being available for their dying. Like Augustine on his deathbed, they may simply wish to be left alone. As anyone knows who has spent time as a patient in a bustling hospital, the tiredness of illness is sometimes increased by strings of well-intentioned people constantly coming and going trying to "help out" by asking "how do you feel?"

Hospice care for another in their living and dying demands that we *pay attention to them,* not giving them the feeling that we would be a lot happier being some place else. Sadly, this is not always the case. Some visit the sick while hanging close to the door. Some people (priests, included) are uncomfortable being with the dying. It is therefore a true blessing for the dying to find someone who can handle their being sick. To find someone who treats dying as an ordinary event can make the person dying feel more at peace with it.

Sometimes this *paying attention* is expressed more by action than by words. My mother spent the last two years of her life dying in a nursing home. She was bed-ridden and mostly out of contact with what we call reality. (When I visited, she often thought I was my long-dead father.) She was beyond theological discussions on life and death. My ministry to her was in bringing the Eucharist (which she somehow understood) and then sitting watching television with her. It was not a terribly momentous act, but I do believe that even in her weakened condition it established some sort of a bond between us. It was a "doing with" that perhaps conveyed the message of "caring about" to her. In any case, she was peaceful and seemed to enjoy it, and what more can you ask for a dying person?

In trying to help our friends exit from this Hospice, it is important that after so many good times in the ballrooms and bedrooms in this Inn where we enjoyed life together, we do not desert them in the lobby as they wait for transportation to take them home. As we sit together, we can remind them of all the good times past. We can make amends for the times we made "not so good" for them. We can point out that (by the grace of God) they are "checking out" without outstanding debts, that their account has been fully covered by the blood of Christ and that a beautiful world awaits them beyond the lobby door. Without saying too much, the very fact that we are willing to sit with them till the end conveys the message that their life is still worth something to us, that we still value it not simply for what it *was* but even for what it *is*. Death in itself carries no special value, but it has *meaning* when the life that is ending is seen to be still valued by another human being.

To minister to the dying, to give them hospice care at the door of death is the greatest sign of love we can show them. It is also one of the most difficult tasks in life, one that must be prepared for with prayer and resolution. I once met a doctor who told me that, along with his usual practice of curing the sick, he selected one terminally ill patient whom he helped to die. When I asked him why he did not try to take care of others, he replied: "I am not strong enough to help more than one at a time." It was a humble admission by one who by profession was a "rescuer," and it was a realistic assessment of what he could and could not do in helping others.

The lesson I took from that experience was that we must be filled with life to help the dying believe in life, and we have only so much life to give. It is a great thing to be able to help someone exit this life at peace, but to do so we must be at peace ourselves, truly believing in the wonder of the beautiful life that exists just beyond the door of this Inn for Travelers.

| PART THREE |

LIFE AFTER DEATH

We did not become Christians in order to obtain the good things of this life, but to obtain that goodness that God promised us in the next. Just now our minds are too limited to perceive what has been promised. No one can show you what you are going to be like when that promise is fulfilled. In this we are like a new-born baby lying in its crib, needing someone else's help for everything. Let's suppose it could understand the words if someone said to it: "Hey, baby, just as you see me walking, doing things, speaking, in a few years this is the way you will be!" Well, that baby would look at itself and then at the grown-up speaking to it and even though it could understand what was being promised, it would not believe it. That's the way we are now, lying here like infants in the feebleness of this flesh. We are promised something tremendous but are unable to see it. And so our faith is stimulated to believe what we do not yet see in order that we may eventually deserve to see what we now believe. (*Sermon 127, 1*)

After-Life: Desires and Dreams

I know that you just love being alive and that you don't ever want to die. You would like to pass from this life to a full life after death without the need for resurrection. While remaining alive you would like to move to a life that is even better. That's what you would really like to happen and I think that every human would agree with you. Indeed, this desire is so universal that it seems engraved on the very foundation of our human nature. (*Sermon 344, 4*)

My doctor told me the other day that I am going to die. It was my spiritual doctor (St. Augustine) who told me this, saying: "As soon as you begin to live you begin to die" (*City of God*, 13.10). His announcement did not surprise me. Once you are in your eighth decade, your slowly deteriorating body predicts your ultimate demise and you begin to look forward to the next adventure, most adventures in this life having become somewhat tiring.

My medical doctor recently hinted at the same message. Of course, his words were not as direct as Augustine's warning. All he said (with a note of surprise) was that my heart was quite good considering my age and size. It was analogous to what the garage mechanic told me sometime earlier when he reported that my car had passed inspection but that I should not plan on taking any long trips.

Because we are so certain that someday we will die, most of us would like to be just as certain about what comes after life. Is there life after death? When our time comes to leave this Hospice, are we moving to "something" or to oblivion? I, for one, would like to be sure of an "after-life," but unfortunately there is no uncontrovertible scientific proof for it. Such a proof depends on experience, and few would claim to have had the experience of an "outside" beyond the doors of this life. Even those who claim to have had such an experience are not much help to me. I have never had the experience of going through the doors of this Inn and then returning. Unlike the room where I write these words, there is no window through which I can see what is outside. I can only believe that there is an "outside" and hope that I am not deceived. I must make a "leap of faith" to believe in my immortality.

I can understand why some of my fellow travelers have been unable to make that leap. Some great thinkers (e.g., Plato and Augustine) have tried to develop arguments from the experience of the "self" for its immortality, but to be honest, the assumptions and the conclusions of the arguments seem far from coercive. They were *cogent* but not *convincing*. They did not give me the same certainty about after-death that I have about before-death.

Even Augustine had his doubts about the strength of his argument. In his youth he devoted a whole book *(On the Immortality of the Soul)* to the subject but upon reviewing the work as an old man he ruefully admitted:

> Because of the intricacy and brevity of its argument, it is so obscure that I can't keep my attention focused on it and, when I am finally able to concentrate on it, I can barely understand what I have done. (*Retractions*, 1.5.1.)

Even if there were a coercive proof for the immortality of the soul, it would not be enough for me! I want my "me" to exist forever and not simply "my soul." I am not so "spiritual-ized" that I accept "my soul" as my "me." For me, the "me" is that thing that lumbers through life now, the "me" that thinks and dreams and reasons and hopes but also gets hungry and gets tired and needs sleep. Convinced that I am body *and* soul, I face the same problem in searching for an after-life as those who believe that the "person" is *only* the body. For them and for me, given the obvious destruction of the body at death, the only three alternatives for an after-life are some sort of "shadow" exist-ence of my now ethereal person, a reincarnation into a new body, or the resurrection of a glorified body. Apart from these three possibilities, the only alternative would seem to be oblivion.

For some (for example, the ancient Epicureans) oblivion after death was not something to worry about. Before death you are alive and hopefully enjoying it; after death you do not suffer because the "you" no longer exists. Along the same lines the great Eastern religions sought not the salvation of the in-dividual but its elimination. In Hindu philosophy individual existence is evil and the cause of human suffering. Therefore the individual must quiet all desires and deny the "self" in order to be absorbed into the Brahman, the first principle. For Buddhism the final goal is a complete negation of the self. This is Nirvana, the only remedy for human pain. In both of these religions, if the ultimate goal was not achieved in one lifetime, there would be a series of reincarnations until the goal of obliv-ion or destruction of the self was achieved.

I may be self-centered, but I'm sorry, the goal of oblivion of my "self" or its absorption into a Universal Being does not satisfy my deepest desires. Oblivion does not seem to me to be an attractive goal despite its freedom from suffering. For me the prospect of oblivion does not take away the desire, the hope, the dream of forever living a pleasant, enjoyable life. I believe that most of us have a similar passion for living. Given the op-tion of oblivion or a fulfilled eternal life, most of us would choose the latter. Even those folks who choose suicide do so not so much to reject life as to get rid of a bad one. Sometimes we are tempted to embrace death not because we are tired of life, but because we are tired of *this* life and deep down hope for something better (*On Freedom of the Will*, 3.7.20–3.8.23).

So strong is this desire to live that some psychologists (e.g., Freud) have even suggested that in our "unconscious" we are convinced that we will indeed live forever. Even if this were so, in our conscious moments there is still a lingering doubt. As Augustine suggests in the opening passage, what we would really like is to pass from life to life without having to go through death, but at very least we would like to be assured that there is life after death.

Apparently the primitive people who lived a half-million years ago did not believe that death was that inevitable. Living on average only eighteen years, they had little or no experience with "natural death." Death for them seemed to come only through some accident or violent attack. In a story that is somewhat like the Genesis description of Eden, they believed that humans were naturally immortal and died only as the result of catastrophe. For them life after death was not a particularly happy life nor would it be forever. Both the good and bad lived a ghostly existence in a land of shadows, finally passing out of existence unless they were reincarnated in a different form.

It is hard to see how the prospect of such a life could bring happiness. Most humans would be satisfied only by a permanent state where the whole "me" (not part of the "me") could enjoy the satisfaction of all its desires. Most humans would not be satisfied by the assurance that after death they would have no desires and hence could not be disappointed. I for one could not be satisfied with oblivion; I want an eternal, vibrant life, a life that has all of the joys and none of the sorrows of this life! Augustine seems to agree. One day he told his listeners:

> Whatever it's like, this life is sweet, and nobody wants to end it, wretched though it is. What must a blessed life be like con-

sidering that we cannot help loving this one with all its miseries: its disappointments, its toil, its sickness, its real sadness, its phony cheerfulness, its prayers for relief, its fear of temptation and tribulation. Who can possibly have the eloquence to adequately describe the sometime wretchedness of this life? But we love it all the same. (*Sermon 335B*, 3)

Loving this life with all its imperfection, we dream and hope for a life that is even better, which indeed is perfect, perfect because it permanently satisfies all our desires (*The Trinity*, 13.8.11).

Islam, Judaism, and Christianity all hold out the possibility of a happy eternal life. We live out our days on earth and then die, entering an eternal life where we are rewarded or punished for the good and evil we have freely chosen here on earth. Despite the terror of possibly being punished forever, I find the prospect of such eternal life consoling. Believing in immortality, I at least have a chance for eternal happiness once I have exited this Hospice through the door of death.

Resurrection

In the fifth century Augustine told his parish congregation:

> When you die your flesh will be stripped away for a while but will come back to you at the end of time. This is going to happen whether you like it or not. You are not going to rise from the grave because you want to; nor will your "not wanting to" prevent it from happening. Even if you don't believe in your eventual resurrection, you will still rise from the grave "willynilly." (*Sermon 344*, 4)

———

Augustine's words are consoling to me because I am one of those who would like to rise from the dead. The assurance of ancient Greeks like Socrates and Plato that my soul will live forever is all well and good, but it is not enough to make me look forward to my after-life experience. Nor is their advice on how to achieve a good after-life too consoling. Their exhortation to purify the mind, increase knowledge, and reach out for sublime wisdom is not too attractive to ordinary "clods" like me. Their heaven seems to be reserved for the intellectual elite while the rest of us are destined to swim through various stages of reincarnation in the "cave" below.

In order to make me happy, I need assurance that after death I will continue to exist "with" my body. I want my body to be with me in eternal life because (as Augustine remarks): "The soul loves life and hates death and because (as Paul says) it doesn't 'hate its own flesh' (Eph 5:29), it does not want death to happen even to its body" (*Sermon 344,* 4). Furthermore, for me to be happy now I need to know that the comfort of my after-life does not depend on how smart I am. It is hard enough for me make sense out of the confusion of my life in this Hospice. To demand a high "I.Q." to get into the good life beyond the doors of this Inn is too much to ask.

If I had to leave this old body behind forever when I pass through the doors of this Hospice, it would be like checking out of a hotel and being told to leave all baggage behind. I would leave with sadness if I could not take with me that precious possession (my body) which was such an important part of my pleasure during my days here. Leaving, I would feel naked and apprehensive because I was forced to leave part of myself behind with no assurance that I would ever see it again. My body may not be the most important part of me, but over seven decades I have gotten used to it, and now it is hard to imagine living without it. I am not consoled when a friend assures me that my body will be sent along later. How can this happen? How can any human being know where to send my body when I leave this life in death? To believe that someone can do this amazing thing is like sending all my earthy goods out into the darkness without insurance.

Since we must leave behind our body at death, we would like to be confident that someday we will regain it. Unfortunately, no one can scientifically prove this will happen to us, because no one can give us the experience before it happens. As Augustine observes, we are familiar with people being born and people dying, but none of us are familiar with the experience of our rising from the dead and living forever (*Sermon 229H,* 1). We believe that Jesus Christ did this long ago for himself, but we did not witness that resurrection and even if we had, the experience would have been of his resurrection, not ours.

Indeed, all experience seems to argue against our rising from the grave. The body deteriorates after death and finally disappears. There may be a way of proving the continuity between this old decrepit body that I have now and the fresh newly-minted body that emerged from my mother's womb so many years ago, but there is no way of establishing such continuity between the body that disappears in the grave and the "new" body that resurrection assumes is "reformed" or "re-created" and reunited to my soul at the end of time. The only way we can be sure that someday we shall rise again is by believing in the *promise* of someone who has the *power* to do it. For the Christian that person is Jesus Christ, and our conviction comes from the deeds Jesus did and the promises he made as recorded by the Christian community in the New Testament.

Christ's *power* over death was demonstrated by a number of incidents that occurred during his time on earth. First and foremost, there was his own resurrection (Luke 24; Matt 28; Mark 16; John 20). Added to this are the various times when he brought ordinary humans back from the grave: Lazarus the brother of Martha and Mary (John 11:1-44); the son of the widow of Naim (Luke 7:11-17); the daughter of Jairus, the Roman centurion (Mark 5:35-43; Luke 8:49-56)

It is in the midst of the story of Lazarus that we find the clearest *promise* that resurrection will be part of our destiny. As the story goes, Jesus went to the house of the sisters of Lazarus (Martha and Mary) some days after his burial. Seeing him, Martha cried out: "Lord, if you had been here, our brother would not have died!" Of course, she was mistaken. Jesus never promised any human (except perhaps Mary, his mother) that they would never die. What he did promise was that when we die we will still live and that the day will come when we will once again live soul and body eternally. His words are simple and direct: "I am the resurrection and the life; whoever believes in me, even if he dies, will live, and everyone who lives and believes in me will never die." And to prove that he had such power over death Jesus then commanded Lazarus to come back from the grave.

That Jesus was serious about this promise is confirmed by the various places where he speaks of resurrection as a certain fact: for example, the parable of the final harvest where the good shall be separated from the bad (Matt 13:37-43); the prophecy of the end of the world where angels go out to collect the chosen (Matt 24:23-31); the discussion with the Sadducees about the status in heaven of the woman who in this life had been married (successively) to seven husbands (Mark 12:18-27); the description of the scene at the end of time (John 5:28-29); and finally, Jesus' moving promise to his followers at the Last Supper: "Do not let your hearts be troubled. I am going to prepare a place for you, and then I shall come back to take you with me, that where I am you also may be" (John 14:1 and 3).

Such stories and many others that were never written down but lived in the memory and tradition of the early Christian community led St. Paul to make the most straightforward declaration of our final resurrection to the Christians at Corinth. He said to them:

> Tell me, if Christ is preached as raised from the dead, how is it that some of you say there is no resurrection of the dead? If there is no resurrection of the dead, Christ himself has not been raised. And if Christ has not been raised, our preaching is void of content and your faith is empty too. If the dead are not to be raised from the grave, then Christ did not rise from the grave; and if Christ was not raised, your faith is worthless and those who have fallen asleep in Christ are the deadest of the dead. If our hopes in Christ are limited to this life only, we are the most pitiable of men. (1 Cor 15:12-19)

Paul's message is clear: for Christians the belief in the immortality of the soul after death and the final resurrection is at the very core of their faith.

Commenting on this four centuries later, Augustine told his people:

The resurrection of the Lord Jesus Christ is the distinctive mark of the Christian faith. Christ says to us:

> "What were you afraid of, you people whom I created and then did not abandon? The ruin in the universe is your doing; its creation was mine! Why are you afraid of dying? Look, I died; look, I suffered. You should not be afraid. I have shown you what to hope for."

There you are, that's exactly what Jesus did. He gave us a demonstration of what it is like to be resurrected for all eternity. The resurrection of Christ is both the distinguishing mark and the foundation of our faith as Christians. (*Sermon 229H*, 1 and 3)

There are, of course, many mysteries involved in the process of our final resurrection, things we cannot understand and will never understand until we go through the process for ourselves. For example, after so many years of deterioration in the grave, how can we be sure that what we get back will be "our" body? Augustine seems sure that it will be truly ours. Commenting on Paul's words (Romans 7) that "I do not put off the flesh forever, but I put it aside for a time," Augustine insists: "I do not put off this earthy body, and receive a brazen body or an ethereal body, I receive the same body . . . *this* body, but now no longer perishable" (*Sermon 256, 2*).

But how can it happen if this old body of mine has decayed and disappeared into the earth? Augustine responds by saying, "Why worry?" Cannot God bring us back from dust when he originally created us from nothing? As he told the people in his church:

> The doubter objects, "But look, what I see in the tomb are cinders, ashes, and bones. How will this pile of dirt once more receive life, skin, tissues, flesh and rise again?" I answer: "At least in the tomb you can see cinders, you can see bones; in your mother's womb there was nothing. Before you existed, there were neither cinders nor bone; and yet you were made, when you did not exist at all. Do you really think that it is impossible that your

bones will receive the form they *used to have,* when at conception you received a form you *never had* before?" (*Sermon 127,* 15)

Perhaps this question about the continuity between my body now and my resurrected body at the end of time is not all that important. Possession will make that glorified body as much mine as is my present somewhat "tattered" body. It is similar to the time when I disposed of my old car to get a new one. The new shiny vehicle I will get at resurrection will be truly mine, and I will not be in the least disturbed that the historical connection with my old wheels is lacking.

The message of Christianity that someday we shall rise again gives us great hope as we live out our dying life just now. We want to live and we want to live forever happy, body and soul. The resurrection of Christ gives us that hope, the hope that we, too, can rise one day to a blessed life. We know this will happen because he has shown us that he has the power over death, and he has promised that he will use that power to bring us back whole and entire at the end of time. As Augustine assured his people long ago:

> Great indeed the power by which Jesus was able not to die; but greater still was the loving kindness by which he was willing to die. The reason, you see, he did by loving kindness what he was also able by power not to do, was to lay for us the foundation for belief in our own resurrection. He wanted to show that the perishable, mortal element that he took upon himself for our sakes would be able to rise again. He did this so that we might hope to do the same thing. Indeed, after his resurrection he ate and drank with his friends to show them what a glorified body was like. (*Sermon 362,* 12)

Our faith in the reality of Jesus and his rising from the dead is the foundation for our hope that someday the same thing will happen to us. We know that it will happen because Jesus Christ, the Son of God, has promised it.

The Possibility of Heaven

In his *The Genius of Christianity* Chateaubriand suggested that for most human beings it is easier to believe in hell than in heaven. He writes that "heaven, where boundless felicity reigns, is too far above the human condition for the soul to be strongly affected by the bliss of the elect; one can interest oneself but little in beings who are perfectly happy."[1]

He has a point. Considering our lack of experience with eternal "blessedness," can we ever be convinced that it is more than a fantasy? Why have human beings come to believe that there is a heaven *beyond* earth when their daily experience is that there is no heaven *on* earth? How can we be sure that our word "Utopia" for the land of eternal blessedness is not sadly predictive? On our bad days a heavenly land of blessedness seems to be truly "no place."

Asking whether heaven is real goes much further than asking whether there is life after death. As we have seen in the reflection on "After-Life," the belief in some sort of continuing existence after death seems to have been a conviction of the human race from earliest times. The belief that this existence could be a "happy existence" developed much later and in its earliest stages was reserved for heroes and other outstanding individuals. For ordinary folks life after death was at best a shadow existence in a land of darkness.

Thus, the Sheol of ancient Judaism and the Hades of ancient Greek religions were indeed places for the dead, but the quality of life there left much to be desired. In Greek mythology the heroic Achilles, living now in the darkness of Hades, cries out: "Don't speak to me placidly about death, O great Odysseus. I would rather live upon earth as the slave of another, a landless man with no great livelihood, than be king of all the departed dead" (*Odyssey*, book XI, 488–81). Along the same lines the beleaguered Job in the Old Testament pleads:

> Are not the days of my life few? Let me alone that I may recover a little before I go to that place from which I shall not return, that land of darkness and of gloom, that black disordered land where darkness is the only light. (Job 10:20-22)

The recognition of a personal resurrection to a land of joy did not appear with any force in the Old Testament until about the second century before Christ in the writings of the Maccabean period. It is only then that we hear sentiments like those expressed in the book of Daniel:

> Many of those who sleep in the dust of the earth shall awake. Some shall live forever; others shall live in everlasting horror and disgrace. But the wise shall shine brightly like the splendor of the firmament, and those who lead the many to justice shall be like the stars forever. (Dan 12:2-3)

According to Hick[2] the belief in a happy immortality that was open to all (and not just the outstanding), an immortality that was a reward for the good one has done, developed only after humans came to believe in the value of individual life and the existence of a "God" who had the power to reward or punish the individual for the quality of life they led before death. These two conditions led to a belief that there was such a thing as "Justice" where everyone and everything was in its proper place and that responsible agents would receive rewards or punishment depending on whether they freely chose to act in accordance with their nature.

When Christ began his teaching, there was a new direction or at least a new emphasis taken on the reality of heaven.

Without denying the two factors mentioned above that led to the earliest belief in a "blessed heaven" for those who "deserved" it, Christ preached a new message. He did not deny that every human had a personal responsibility for their actions nor that God was a God of Justice who would reward or punish the individual for their deeds, but he emphasized more that God was a God of Love. God created human beings not because he wanted someone to judge but because he wanted someone who could choose to love him and be with him happily for all eternity.

Because God was a God of Love, humans were not left to their own devices. God reached down and lovingly gave them the strength to do what they had to do to have a blessed eternity. Christ did not tell his followers to spend their time analyzing the minutiae of law lest they fail in their observance and therefore be judged unworthy. He told them to try their best (with the help of God) to "love God above all and love each other as they love themselves."

Later on Augustine would simplify the command even further by telling his friends that what this command of love was saying was: "Love and do what you will." That is, if a person loves creation, self, neighbor and God in the proper way, or at least *tries* to love well, that is all that is required to achieve a "blessed" eternal heaven (*Commentary on the First Epistle of John*, 7.8).

This message of love and understanding of weakness was especially important for Augustine. After trying to cure his guilt about his life through the hopelessness of Manicheanism ("Nothing you do is your fault"), the agony of skepticism ("Nothing matters that much"), the cold spiritual immortality of the Platonists ("Your soul can be saved but not your 'self'"), he finally came to believe in Jesus-God and through Jesus' promises he became convinced that a real heaven existed, a warm heaven that embraced his whole person (soul and body), a state of blessedness which even he with all his past faults and present weakness could perhaps enjoy one day. Through the gift of his faith, he came to believe that God out of love had entered human history in the person of Jesus Christ and that this Incarnate God out of love had promised a blessed eternity to those who had tried their best in this life to love God and each other. Because of this faith he would later joyfully declare to his friends: "We can be certain that what has been promised will come true because it is Christ himself who has promised it" (*Commentary On Psalm 122,* 9).

Believing that Christ was God, Augustine needed only to search the Gospel to find the promises that this God had made. Reflecting on the story of the Transfiguration, he told the people in his church:

> What he promised to those who love him will find its fulfillment there (in heaven). Jesus told his friends: "Whoever loves me will be loved by my Father, and I too will love him." Then, as if someone had asked him, "What will you give such a human who loves you, seeing that you will return that love?" he answers "I will show myself to him!" (John 14:21) What a tremendous gift! what a wonderful promise! God is not giving some special reward to those who love him; he is giving himself! (*Sermon 78,* 5).

This promise of eternally possessing God was repeated again and again in the New Testament. We find Jesus telling the thief Dismas on Calvary: "This day you will be with me in paradise" (Luke 23:43). He promises his friends: "Whoever loses his soul for my sake will find it in eternal life" (Matt 8:35); "Blessed are the pure of heart for they will see God" (Matt 5:8). Finally, in his very last conversation with his disciples at the Last Supper, Jesus tells them:

> Do not let your hearts be troubled. Have faith in God and faith in me. In my Father's house there are many dwelling places; otherwise, how could I have told you I was going to prepare a place for you? I am indeed going to prepare a place for you, and

then I shall come back to take you with me, that where I am you also will be. (John 14:1-3)

For those who believe in the promises of Jesus-God, the one certainty in the midst of this ever-moving life is that heaven exists and is a blessed existence where it is possible for every human being to enjoy unending life in the presence of God. To paraphrase Paul's words to the Corinthians (1 Cor 15:16-17), if heaven is not real then our faith is indeed worthless because "if our hopes in Christ are limited to this life only, we are indeed the most pitiable of all human beings" (1 Cor 15:19).

NOTES

1. Quoted in the *Oxford Book of Death*, D. J. Enright, ed. (New York: Oxford University Press, 1983) 179.

2. John H. Hick, *Death and After-Life* (San Francisco: Harper and Row, 1976) 63–64.

What Will Heaven Be Like?

Once assured that heaven is a reality, that there is a "blessed state" that awaits us when we exit this Hospice, we naturally begin to try to figure out what such a heaven might be like. Unfortunately, whatever we say just proves that we don't know what we are talking about. As Sir Thomas Browne wrote long ago, any discussion about the nature of the happy world that awaits us beyond the doors of this Hospice is like two infants in the womb speculating about what life is like outside.[1] Our words about life in heaven, like panel discussions at philosophy conventions, usually have little to do with reality. As Augustine told his people: "Only those who experience it can know what such a life is like and only those who believe in it will ever be able to have that experience" (*Sermon 259*, 1).

Of course, such warnings have never stopped us from dreaming. From the days of the "Egyptian Book of the Dead" (written in 3300 B.C.), through Buddhism's "Description of the Happy Land," the New Testament book of Revelation, the Koran of Islam, and the *Divine Comedy* of Dante, we humans have never been able to resist imagining the joys that await us once we reach that blessed land that is called "heaven." Despite Paul's warning that the "eye has not seen, ear has not heard, nor has it so much as dawned on man what God has prepared for those who love him" (2 Cor 2:9), we go on dreaming anyway. It was such dreaming that led Isaiah to prophesy what the "heaven on earth" would be like when God finally returned to make Israel triumphant. He hears God saying: "No longer shall the sound of weeping be heard or the sound of crying. No longer shall there be in it an infant who lives but a few days or an old man who does not round out the full days of his life" (Isa 65:19-20).

When we think about what heaven will be like, we usually begin by listing what we "want." We reason that if we cannot be happy when we "want" something, then heaven must be a place where we will possess whatever we want. In eternity we will finally possess all those good things that we wanted but could not obtain on our pilgrimage through time (*Commentary on Psalm 37*, 28). Such thinking about what we "want" does no harm as long as it does not distract from what we really "need" in order to be perfectly satisfied, needs like

1. the need to *live* and to live at the peak of all our human powers;
2. the need to realize that our lives *mean* something, that they have *value;*
3. the need for *love,* to care for and be cared about by another person;
4. the need for the *freedom* to determine our destiny.

Because these needs are rooted in our nature we cannot eliminate them by doing away with them. With some effort a smoker may overcome addiction to nicotine, but no one can overcome their addiction to living and loving.

We know that if heaven means anything, it at least means that all these natural desires will be eternally satisfied. The blessedness of heaven must include the perfect and permanent satisfaction of these desires because they are not just goods that we "want" but are goods that we truly "need" to become fulfilled. We need life, meaning, love, and freedom to be filled out as a person, to be completed. To be fulfilled does not mean that we have everything we could possibly want. Rather, it is to have what we truly "need" and to "want" nothing that we really don't need.

But how is such perfect fulfillment to be achieved? The message of Sacred Scripture is that this "filling up" of self is achieved only through the act of love, the "reaching out" towards a good we do not have and the delight in the good that we do have. It is love that drives us towards good yet to be possessed and makes us rejoice in good already embraced. Put simply, heaven is the complete fulfillment of self through the perfect receiving and giving of love.

Love is not a passive act, an inert basking in love received. Fulfillment comes from giving love, having it received and then returned by the object of our affection. We cannot be "filled up" by sitting quietly while someone "pumps" their love into us as though they were filling up our car with gasoline. We are filled by immersing ourselves in the loved one, by diving in with our whole self, holding nothing back, submerging ourselves in the good that is the lovely "other." This is the clear message that Christ preaches. It is only through such reciprocal love that we can reach that state of blessedness where our "self" is completed by being united with and possessing all that it loves.

It is obvious that this does not happen in this life. As long as we are in this Hospice, we are limited by the "crackedness" that makes it impossible for us to give and receive love perfectly. In this life our "self" is always incomplete and thus incapable of perfect "blessedness." We may have some blessed moments, but they do not last long. Just now we are not capable of producing that perfect "giving away of self" that is the only path to fulfillment.

Christ's statement that "whoever would save his life will lose it, and whoever loses his life for my sake will save it" (Luke 9:24) tells us that if we selfishly wrap ourselves up in our own "self" and do not offer love to others, we will be forever narrow and incomplete. It is only through reaching out to the good beyond us (that is, loving it) that we can prepare to be filled up and perfected. Giving our love empties us so that there is room for God's love to flood in and take over our lives. Striving for that perfect giving of self through love prompted Augustine to cry out: "O to love! To go and be lost to self! To reach God! (*Sermon 159*, 8).

Is this just silly romanticism? Is not a life characterized only by "loving" a terribly narrow existence? Is it not like being trapped on a desert island with only one book to read and that a romantic novel? Augustine answers that it is hard to make a person who has never been in love understand what it means when the psalmist says of heaven: "We will be made *drunk* with the fullness of your house and the torrents of the pleasures you will give to drink" (Ps 35:8-10) (*Commentary on the Gospel of John*, 26.4.3). A person who has never loved is just too frozen to understand (*Commentary on Psalm 32/2*, 6). It follows that Augustine's advice to those trying to understand what heaven is like would be very uncomplicated. He would tell them, "Fall in love!"

When you come to think about it, there is merit in this advice. When you fall deeply in love with another human being, the overpowering ecstasy of being in the presence of the loved one, of embracing and being embraced by the person you love, somehow or other makes everything else disappear. You may still be aware of your surroundings, but now they seem different. Now they are bathed in the light of your love and seem brighter and more refreshing. It is like walking in early morning along a quiet beach holding hands with a loved one. The sky somehow seems bluer. The songs of the seabirds seem sweeter. The air sweeps over you like fine wine and the aroma of the sea suddenly becomes intoxicating. Such an experience is a small hint of what heaven will be like when we are embraced forever by our Divine and human loves.

The necessary and sufficient cause of our joy in heaven will come from perfectly possessing and being possessed by God. As Augustine puts it, we will be "glued to God" (*Commentary on Psalm 62*, 17). Like someone overcome with the delight of a good wine, we will want nothing more. We will be "drunk with God" (*Commentary on Psalm 35*, 14). God will be everything we ever wanted. As Augustine describes our happy state: "With him you will possess all that is; you will have it all, and he will have all there is of you" (*Commentary on Psalm 36/1*, 12). To those who still seem to want more, he cries out in exasperation: "You greedy misers, what will ever satisfy you if God himself does not satisfy you?" (*Sermon 19, #5*).

Though all will be equally "blessed" in heaven, we will be unequal in our capacity to love. Though we will all be "stars," not all of us will be "super-novas." But we will be satisfied nonetheless. We will not be like spoiled children anxiously and loudly demanding the full (and hopefully exclusive) attention of our heavenly Father. We will not be like we are sometimes in this life, jealous that our beloved happens to love others too. We will rejoice in our differences because (despite our different capacities) we will all be *full*. Like a child at a Thanksgiving table, we will not be upset by the vast appetite of the "grown ups" who feast on much more than we can contain. We will happily munch on our little bone while they continue to gorge themselves on larger quantities of the bird. We will be happy because we, like them, will be *full*. In heaven we will rejoice in being a member of the happy Mystical Body and not be disturbed that we are only a humble finger. As Augustine says:

> It would be as foolish for the lower to long to be higher as it would be for a finger to crave to be an eye. The great gift of those enjoying a more humble state in heaven will be that they will long for nothing more. (*City of God*, 22.30)

The love and enjoyment of God will be the most important part of our bliss, but we will also rejoice in loving and being loved by those around us. Indeed (as some have suggested), we will love God in and through the precious human loves that are with us in eternity.[2] United with our loves and with them embraced by the love of God, never again will we weep for someone who may leave us and never again will we worry about someone who has yet to come (*Commentary on the Gospel of John*, 32.9.3).

In this life our thoughts are sometimes dominated by anxiety about those we love, wondering what they are doing, hoping that they are at peace. Such anxiety will not exist when we are all together in heaven. There we will know that they are at peace and that they will be at peace forever (*City of God*, 19.13).

Our experience of perfect love in heaven will bring perfect joy because it will satisfy all of the natural desires mentioned above. With respect to our desire for life, it is true that in our present condition love does not guarantee good health. Being in love does not stop us from dying. But anyone who has been deeply in love with another human being must admit that life is enriched, that somehow or other you "feel better." When you are terribly sick or dying, love from another will not cure you or save you, but it can make your dying life a bit brighter. For most of us even a life that is eternal would not be attractive if we were all alone.

Loving and being loved certainly helps fulfill our desire for meaning. It is easier to be convinced that our life means something when it means something to someone else. It takes a strong (or self-centered) person to believe that they are important in the scheme of things when everyone else thinks that they are worth nothing. In heaven when we come to realize how important we are in the eyes of God, we can have no doubt that our life means something because we will see that it means something to an infinite lover. We will be able to see clearly for the first time what it is in us that God loves. We will see that all the time we have been vessels carrying the image of our Divine Lover. As a result:

> In heaven true honor will never be denied where it is due. Since none but those who are worthy will be there, no one will unworthily desire their proper glory. (*City of God*, 22.30)

It is obvious that loving and being loved will fulfill our desire for love. The only mystery is how this love can become perfect in heaven when it is often so imperfect in this life. The answer is that our love will become perfect because we will finally realize that we are loved eternally with an infinite love and that at last we are able to return that love as perfectly as our natural limits permit.

But how can love, even perfect love, satisfy our natural desire to be free? It would seem that when we are bound to another by love, we are less free. But is this the case? If freedom is nothing more than the power to choose what we want to choose, is it not true that when we are deeply in love with another, we would never choose anything other than to love them? Indeed, in the ecstasy that comes with being united with our love, we are not able to think about anything or anyone else.

The freedom of heaven is like that. In the presence of the Infinite Good that is God, there is no other good to tempt our choice. Even our continuing love for our human and angelic friends will not be an obstacle. We will choose them not instead of God but because of God, because of the reflected brilliance of the divinity in them that we now are able to see clearly for the first time. We will be free because we will choose the one and only good that we want to choose, the Infinite Good that is God. Bathed in such infinite love, "there will remain in each and all of us an inalienable freedom of the will, emancipating us from every evil and filling us with every good" (*City of God*, 22.30). We will be able to live as we want because our overpowering love will not permit us to "want" anything beyond God (*The Trinity*, 13.7.10).

As a result of giving and receiving love, we shall finally be able to enjoy that wonderful rest that was enjoyed by the first innocent humans in paradise (*Letter 55*, 9, 16–17). Finally and forever, there will be a stillness like the stillness we sometimes experience as we doze in the arms of our beloved waiting for the dawn (*City of God*, 22.30.4-5). We will remember the past but without anxiety (*City of God*, 22.30). We will be at peace, no longer at war with others or with ourselves (*Enchiridion: Faith, Hope, Charity*, 23.91). In heaven we shall finally and forever be friends with our old body now renewed and refurbished (*Sermon 155*, 14; *City of God*, 22.30).

The restfulness of heaven does not mean that we will tire of our immortality (*Sermon* 211A). Indeed, we will be vibrantly active, enthusiastically shouting "Alleluia" and "Amen" at the top of our lungs. When Augustine first told his congregation this, they became restless, perhaps mumbling to themselves: "Boring! Boring!" (*Sermon 243*, 9.8). He eased their fears by explaining what the words meant. He told them that shouting "Amen!" was like crying out

> So THAT'S the answer! That's what the universe is like and what I am like and what God is like! Now I KNOW! Now I have finally figured out what life is about! Everything I ever wanted to know, I now know!

The cry "Alleluia" is also a cry of joy, shouting with the full force of our being "PRAISE GOD!" as we are inflamed with love for the reality of the God whom we now see clearly for the first time (*Sermon 362*, 29). Such enthusiastic cheering is but the natural response to our awareness of God's infinite love and our easy, burdenless, untiring participation in that love.

Augustine summed up the experience of heaven for his friend Proba:

> There the days do not come and go in succession, and the beginning of one day does not mean the end of another. All days are one, simultaneously and without end. The wonderful life we shall live on that day will never end. (*Letter 130*, 8.15)

What he was saying to her was: "It will be indeed a WONDERFUL time and best of all, my dear, it will NEVER END!"

NOTES

1. Sir Thomas Browne, quoted in *Oxford Book of Death*, D. J. Enright, ed. (New York: Oxford University Press, 1983) 171.

2. Michael P. Morris, "Afterlife" in *The New Dictionary of Catholic Spirituality*, M. Downey, ed. (Collegeville: Liturgical Press, 1993) 29.

The Sad Necessity for Hell

We know for sure that someday we will leave this Hospice that is our temporary dwelling just now. The question is "leave to what?" Sometimes in my travels here on earth (usually to a convention of philosophers), the meetings were held in a downtown hotel in the midst of a dark "tenderloin" district that was dangerous to roam even in the daylight. In such a situation staying inside seemed to be the best plan. Outside was darkness and danger and terror. I knew that I had to leave someday (even seemingly endless philosophy conventions must end) and throughout my stay I spent a good bit of my time anxiously planning my leaving so as to spend the least time in that dark, dangerous environment beyond the doors.

Even when I dwelt happily in my favorite motel high on Bass Rocks just north of Boston, I experienced the same reluctance to leave. What was "outside" indeed seemed heavenly, at least while the sun was still shining. But sometimes in the dark of night while I was in the twilight of my sleep, hearing the thunder of a violent storm crashing the seas against the rocks below, I dreamt of a terrible possibility, the possibility that I would stumble into the darkness outside and blindly plunge over the precipice into the raging sea below.

A similar fear sometimes overcomes me as I think of the day when I must leave this Hospice that is just now the place where I live. My faith promises me that there is a "heaven" outside the doors, a place of everlasting blessedness and joy where the air is always sweet. But it also warns me that there is another place, a place of everlasting darkness and emptiness into which I may tumble because of my stupidity and excesses. Is it possible that, far from being an eternal success, I will become an eternal failure, living in a place of torment with others who have shared my failure as a human being?

It is an especially frightening possibility for those of us who believe in the teachings of Jesus Christ. He makes it clear that, just as the happiness of heaven is caused by an eternal union with God, the suffering of hell is caused by a decision to separate from God forever. Augustine tried to describe the anguish resulting from such a decision. He wrote:

> To lose the kingdom of God, to be an exile from the City of God, to be estranged from the life of God, to be bereft of the great abundance of the sweetness of God, such would be the agony of such eternal punishment that no earthly tortures we experience can be compared with it even if they were unending. (*Enchiridion*, 29.112)

As is the case with heaven (the eternal union with God), to be convinced of the reality of hell (the eternal rejection of God) depends on faith. In this Hospice where we live out our lives just now, we have no experience of what lies beyond the doors. Although the particulars of hell as revealed in the teachings of Christianity, Judaism, and Islam depend on faith, the certainty that some sort of unpleasant existence awaits humans after death seems to have been ingrained in many ancient civilizations. Human beings ended up in these cheerless places, not because they had been evil but simply because they had been human.

It was only later that such a "hellish" existence was reserved for those who before death had lived an evil life. Certainly by the time of Christ, the belief in a *Gehenna* ("hell" as we know it today) was firmly established. Thus, in the Gospel of Matthew we find it described as a place of eternal suffering

(Matt 18:8; 25:41) where the condemned voiced their pain with a "weeping and gnashing of teeth" (Matt 25:30).

This teaching continued in the tradition of Christianity throughout history. As early as the second century St. Justin was teaching that the punishment of the fallen angels and condemned humans without doubt began after the final judgment. In the fifth century Augustine again and again warned his listeners about the terrible "Second Death" that awaited those who had turned their back upon God. For example, in his *City of God*, he writes:

> The doom in store for those who are not of the City of God is an unending wretchedness that is called "the Second Death," because neither the soul, cut off from the life of God, nor the body, pounded by perpetual pain, can be said have a "life" at all. Worse still, what will make that Second Death so hard to bear is that there will be no death to end it. (*City of God, 19.28*)

He repeated the same theme in his sermons, telling his listeners:

> Death should be dreaded but it is after all only a passing event. Would that this first death separating soul from body were the only death. A worse death is that Second Death where the soul is not separated FROM the body, but where the soul is tormented IN the body. Fear this death more because nothing is worse than a death that never dies. (*Sermon 335B, #5*)

Augustine's teaching on the eternity of this Second Death was confirmed in 543 by the Church's condemnation of the position taught by Origen that the torments of hell are only for a time. In 1336 a further clarification was made when the Church solemnly proclaimed (contrary to what Justin had believed) that the punishment of hell begins *immediately* after death.

Today the teaching of Roman Catholicism on the possibility of humans being condemned to hell may be summed up in three statements:

1. God wishes that all humans be saved. This is proven by the fact that Christ died to redeem all human beings without exception.
2. However, this redemption of the whole human race does not mean that there is a guarantee that everyone will be saved. Salvation for the individual depends now on the individual's free choice aided by the grace of God.
3. Though no one knows for sure that any human being is in hell, it remains a terrible possibility for every one of us.

One of the frightening results of the creation of immortal beings with free will is that it made hell a sad necessity. Once granted that human beings have free choice and that in a world created by a just God "Justice must be served," the need for a hell follows. It is evident from experience that human beings do not always act "justly," they do not always act in accordance with their nature. They disrupt the order of the universe by pretending to be God, by not treating fellow humans as equals, by acting as though they were animals bound by no law except the law of self-fulfillment.

Assuming that we have free choice and that some of our actions are determined by that free choice, it is reasonable to reward us for our good choices and to punish us when we choose evil. If freedom means anything, it means that most of us "could do otherwise" than what we actually did do. Acting like a hero, we could have chosen to be cowards. Acting like a brute, we could have chosen to be saints. No one would condemn a pig for acting like a pig or rebuke a lion for sometimes eating its young, but it seems quite appropriate to censure humans for similar acts of bestiality and cruelty. If they had so chosen, they could have acted otherwise.

It is also evident that in this life the virtuous are not always adequately rewarded for the good they do, nor are the vicious always adequately punished for their evil. If justice is to be perfectly served, then there must be places of reward and punishment in an afterlife where the balance of justice can be restored. The glory of freedom is that most of us are able to freely and irrevocably choose God; the tragedy of freedom is that we can just as irrevocably choose to reject God, to turn our back on God and walk away. And this is what hell is: to firmly and forever turn our back upon God.

It is a mystery why anyone would make such a choice. Can a created thing really believe that they can make it on their own, that they are so endowed with gifts of nature that they need depend on no one else? The story of Creation shows that this is exactly what a creature did. The creature was Lucifer, the most perfect of all the angels. Long before humans were given the challenge to make a choice for or against God, Lucifer with full knowledge made such a choice. He cried to God, "I will not serve!" and walked away. God, respecting the immortal free nature that he had created, let him go. He did not annihilate him; he allowed that great angel to walk away to a place where "God was not." This was the beginning of hell.

Why would any creature, especially the "best of the best," make such a terrible decision? There can be only one answer. Seeing the brilliant reflection of God that he found in his own nature, Lucifer (the "light-bearer") came to believe that he was as good as God. It was as though the mirror in the fairy tale, "Snow White," perceiving the beauty of the fair maiden reflected on its surface, would proudly declare: "Look upon my gleaming surface and see that I am as beautiful as you! I do not need your beauty to reflect beauty. I am beauty itself." Hearing such an odd declaration, even the tolerant Snow White would have only one reasonable course of action: dispose of the mirror and choose another that did not have such extraordinary pretentiousness.

Something similar happened to the great angel Lucifer. Seeing the awesome degree of his own goodness, he came to believe that he was all-good. He looked at himself and pridefully proclaimed: "I am as good as God. I can make it on my own, thank you very much." In that assertion he became Satan, the prince of devils, condemned to "make it on his own" for all eternity.

Scripture testifies that humans were given the same gift of free choice that had been given to Lucifer. Those first humans, though as perfect as they could be as humans, could not match the perfection of Lucifer. Both in their ability to know and in their ability to choose freely, humans were limited. But they still had the power to choose to disobey God, and unfortunately this is precisely what they did choose. Luckily, because their choice was not as calculated as Lucifer's, it was not irrevocable. However, it was serious enough to cause the death of the Incarnate Son of God to reverse its effects. Happily, once that amazing redemptive sacrifice had been performed, human destiny was once again placed firmly in our hands. Now, with the help of God, we humans can once again choose God.

Of course, we are not compelled to do so. There remains the terrible possibility that at the end of this life we will freely choose to turn our backs on God and walk away. We do not know if any human being has or will make such an awful choice, but because it is possible, going to hell remains a possibility for us.

Some object that the very existence of an unending hell is contrary to the goodness of God and to his infinite mercy. But is God's goodness not powerfully demonstrated in giving humans a chance to make the right decision? Would his goodness be better demonstrated by treating us as irresponsible "clods," proclaiming: "No matter what you say or do I will force you to enter into heaven, if necessary carrying you 'kicking and screaming' through the 'pearly gates'"?

It seems to me that this would be like saying to a child who has just painted purple streaks on the living room walls: "That's all right. You are too dumb to know what you have done!" Perhaps you are showing kindness to your beloved child in saying this, but you are certainly not showing the child respect. You are saying, "Whatever you do has little importance because you are never responsible for what you do."

It is certainly true that we could not perform any good act without the support of the grace of God. It is equally true God does everything he can to prevent us from doing evil acts. But in both cases it is also true that our freely chosen acts remain ours and that our dignity as human beings demands that we be held responsible for them.

A second objection against the terrible possibility of hell was raised by one of my students. She asked: "Since freedom creates the necessity for hell would it not be kinder to create us without the freedom to choose to reject God?" I responded by pointing out that taking away the freedom to reject God would also take away the power to love God freely and this would frustrate God's purpose in creation. There is a principle in philosophy that reads: *Bonum diffusivum sibi* ("Good has a natural tendency to spread itself far and wide"). Faith tells us that was the reason why creation occurred at all. God who was All-Good wished to extend his love to some who had the opportunity to freely return that love.

Some (like Origen) have objected that it is unfair to have an eternal punishment for a crime committed in time. Punishment should fit the crime, and therefore the punishment of hell should be like purgatory, lasting only until the blemishes caused by past sins are wiped away. But "cleansing" is not what hell is about. It is not a place of "punishment" so much as it is a place for those who have rejected God and thereby rejected heaven, a place for those who lived a sinful life and died an unrepentant death and thereby made the choice to turn their backs on God.

Perhaps a better analogy for humans who end up in hell is not that they are like prisoners in jail paying for their crimes. They are more like the incurably insane confined in an asylum with no hope of ever being released. Those in hell can never ascend to the "City of God" because of their warped nature, a "warping" that they have freely chosen with full knowledge of the consequences.

Our Christian faith assures us that there is a "somewhere" beyond the doors of this Hospice where we live just now, indeed that there are two "somewheres." The good news is that one of these is heaven. The bad news is that the other is hell. The *very* good news is that where we finally end up is within our control. There may be a sad necessity for hell but there is no necessity for us to end up there. Our salvation is in our (and God's) hands and working together we can accomplish it.

The Probability of My Salvation

I know that someday I will die, that the day will come when I must leave this Hospice where I am living out my life just now. I have come to believe in my immortality, that I will not go through the doors of death into oblivion but into a new life that will never end. This "new life" will be either in a heaven (a place of eternal joy) or in a hell (a place of eternal misery), and I believe that which residence will be mine will be determined by my own choice, a choice aided by the grace of God. Now, as I stand looking out through the window of my little room at eternity, I ask myself: "What is the probability that at the end of my life I will make the right choice? What must I do in order to be saved?"

The general answer to this question is more easily expressed as a negative: "To be saved all I must do is 'not choose' to turn my back on God." It seems reasonable to say (since Christ died for all human beings) that salvation is possible for every human being who does not choose to reject it. No one will be denied salvation except those who knowingly and freely choose to reject God. It would therefore follow that, if I am to be saved, I must be a member of one of these groups:

1. Those who have persevered in leading mostly good lives;
2. Those who led mostly evil lives but who (like Dismas) repented before death and asked forgiveness;
3. Those who lack the clarity of mind or freedom of will to make a responsible decision for or against God.[1]

Despite what some may say, at this moment I cannot claim to be part of that last group. I think that I have been responsible for my choices in life up to this point. This may change in the future under the attack of a mental disability or "older" age, but right now I am *compos mentis,* a relatively healthy mind in a deteriorating body. If I am to be saved it will either be as a somewhat tarnished "saint" or as a humbly penitent sinner.

In a sermon to the people of Hippo, Augustine observed that "anyone who lives well is not able to die badly" (*Sermon 249,* 2). Christ outlined what "living well" means when he told his listeners that they must love God above all and love their neighbor as themselves (Matt 23:37-40). This emphasis on "love" makes good sense. In order to "get" to heaven, we must effectively "want" to get there. We must effectively "desire" heaven but to desire it is another way of saying "to love" it. Since heaven is the one and only eternal "place of God," to love heaven always and above all means to love God above all. Therefore, to reach heaven we must "focus on heaven" and do nothing that would cause us to "turn our back on God." If we love in that perfect way, all other moral rules will follow. We will wish for nothing contrary to the will of our Infinite Lover, God.

To "focus on heaven" obviously does not mean that we should go through life with heads upturned, like lunatics constantly "mooning" over the moon. The second part of Christ's "law of love" forbids such indifference to the things and people around us. We may claim that it is hard to know how to love the still unseen God as we should, but it should not be hard for us to know whether we are "loving neighbor as ourselves."

As Augustine learned from his own experience, none of us needs to be commanded to love ourselves. As he told his congregation: "There are no humans who do not love themselves, but there are many who will lose themselves by loving themselves in the wrong way" (*Sermon 179a,* 4). It is easy to love ourselves, but it is sometimes difficult to love ourselves in a "right" way by loving ourselves as a sacred place of God in the world, by taking care of ourselves, by trying to hone and perfect our gifts, by trying to overcome our defects.

Having developed to some degree this "selfless" love of self, we can turn to our neighbor (and, by extension, to all other creatures) and begin to love them as we have loved ourselves: as places of God in this world. We then are beginning to love God "above all" by loving him in his creation. Though involved in earthly matters, our eyes are still focused on God in his heaven but now through the neighbor and the universe that he created out of love and in which he continues to dwell. While still living on earth we are being drawn to the heavens.

Augustine explains in various places how this love of God, this desire for God, expresses itself in action. For example, he wrote to two friends:

> In order to live a life here that will lead to eternal life I know that we must indulge our bodily desires only to the extent that it is necessary to sustain and carry on our life. I know that we must patiently and bravely bear up under the troubles of life for the sake of God's glory and our neighbor's salvation. I know, too, that we must be considerate and love others so that they may live an upright life worthy of eternity. In case of conflict we must be ready to sacrifice carnal needs to those that are spiritual, passing things to those that are everlasting. I am confident that we can accomplish all these things to the extent that we are helped by the grace of God coming to us through Jesus Christ our Lord. (*Letter 95,* #6)

Augustine became even more specific about the meaning of "living well" in a short sermon to the newly baptized. He told them they should begin by being faithful to their marriage vows or whatever other vows they made to God. In business they must avoid fraud and speak the truth. They should avoid excess and talking too much. In general they should not do to others what they would not like done to themselves. He concludes by assuring the newly baptized that if they did only these things, the God of peace would be with them (*Sermon 260*). In another place he adds that the cost of heaven is never more than what a person has (*Commentary on Psalm 49*, 13).

All of these directions on how to be saved are interesting and even helpful, but they don't answer the nagging question: How sure can I be of *my* salvation? How sure can I be that I will have the strength to fulfill the two great commandments of love well enough to get into heaven even though in a slightly "scarred" and perhaps "singed" condition? It is true that through the grace of God I have come to believe in Jesus Christ (even being baptized in his name). I have some vague idea of what I must do to be saved, but what assurance can I have that someday I will not try to hide the truth from myself? What assurance do I have that for the rest of my life I will actually go ahead and do what needs to be done to be saved? The sad fact is that just now I can't be sure. I have been redeemed but I do not yet know whether I am in a "saved" condition or will be so tomorrow. Like Augustine, "I may be able to know to some extent what I am today, but what I shall be tomorrow I do not know" (*Sermon 179*, 10).

It is enlightening but not particularly consoling to learn that God knows what my tomorrow will be like and also what my eternal destiny will be. It is like the time my organic chemistry professor gathered all of us (except for one poor lad) into the corner of the lab and whispered to us, "In two minutes that man's experiment will explode." And so it did, much to our delight (at that moment we were more unkind observers than caring Christians). God has like foreknowledge of my future, what life experiences will explode and which will bear lasting fruit. God knows now whether I will be lost or saved and (as Augustine says) it would be "silly" to say otherwise (*City of God*, 5.9). Indeed, "In God's sight there is nothing that exists as past and future; everything is now" (*83 Diverse Questions*, 17). This foreknowledge of God can be a sobering revelation. Thinking about it too much may tempt us to say:

How can there be a future possibility for me if someone can see my future with the clarity equal to my vision of my present or past? How can I hope for an already foreseen future, a future that will be infallibly actual someday?

The answer is that although God knows our future, we (supported by and influenced by God's grace) are the ones who make it happen.

Augustine's reading of Sacred Scripture led him to conclude that some (indeed, many) humans are not saved, but this opinion has not found a place in the official teaching of the Catholic Church. It is certain that an eternal hell exists and that it is possible for any of us to end up there. But no one knows if any human has ever had the depths of malice that would warrant such a terrible condemnation.[2]

Is any human being capable of making such a momentous decision against God freely and knowingly? What about those who have never experienced love in this life, those who were cruelly abused or discarded? What about those who never knew of Christ, indeed never knew of a personal God who cared about them? Can someone turn their back on the Eternal Light when they have lived their whole life in darkness? Can a blind man be condemned for not embracing a light he has never known? A sad reality of this life is that some humans seem never to have experienced the light that comes from loving and being loved. Can they be condemned, when at the end of life they see no God to embrace?

Are there reasons for hope that such as these will be saved? Are there reasons for hope that we will be saved, we who have been gifted with faith and love but have often wasted those gifts? Augustine suggests that there are good reasons for hope for all of us. First, our God is a God of power and mercy. We may sometimes fear his power, but it is precisely that power that he uses mercifully to prevent us from being tempted overly much or, if we fall to temptation, to encourage us to repent and try again.

There is even a therapeutic effect coming from our battles. It is only when we are challenged that we learn our true strengths and weakness (*Commentary on Psalm 61*, 20).

Furthermore, our hope is founded on the life and death of Jesus Christ. Augustine explains:

> Christ has become our hope by being tempted, by suffering, by rising again. That is how he has become our hope; for what do we say to ourselves when we read about these happenings? We say:
>
>> God surely won't damn us in the end, since it was for us that he sent his Son to be tempted, to be crucified, to die, and to rise again. God cannot despise us, if he did not spare even his own Son, but delivered him up for the sake of us all. (cf. Rom 8:32)
>
> That is how he has become our hope. He made himself a pattern for the life we live now by his labors, his temptations, his sufferings, and his death; and in his resurrection he is the pattern for the life we will live later. Without him, all that we would have known of human life is that we are born and we die; we would not have known that anyone could rise from the dead and live forever. But he took upon himself the human lot you know, and gave you proof of what you did not know. This is why he has become our hope in distress and in temptation. (*Commentary on Psalm 60*, #4)

Perhaps the greatest reason for our hope for heaven is that we need not be perfect to get in, just repentant. Towards the end of his life Augustine got into a debate with a group who insisted that even the least sin could condemn us to hell. Augustine (perhaps remembering his own blemished life) angrily replied that if that were the case, no one would ever make it! He went on to give a description of the ordinary people who someday were likely to be saved:

> They are those who, with faith in Christ, are moved by his love to perform whatever good works they do. Some are ordinary married persons who have intercourse with their spouse (but never

with anyone else) sometimes for the sake of having a child and sometimes just for the pleasure of it. They are people who will often get angry and desire revenge when they are injured, but who are ready to forgive when asked. They are people who are very attached to their property but who will freely give at least a modest amount to the poor. They will not steal from you but are quick to take you to court if you try to steal from them. They are realistic enough to know that God should get the main credit for the good that they do. They are humble enough to admit that they are the source of their own evil acts. In this life God loves them for their good acts and gives forgiveness for their evil, and in the next life they will join the ranks of those who will reign with Christ forever. (*Against Two Letters of the Pelagians*, 3, 5, 14)

Augustine is simply repeating the message of the book of Revelation (7:14) that those who will eventually be saved and march into heaven will be "those who have survived the great period of trial, those who have washed their robes and made them white in the blood of the Lamb." I do believe that if the observer had asked God why these people limping into heaven had merited salvation, he would have heard the response: "They were not perfect nor did they clearly see what they should do, but at least they tried their best." With God's help I hope to be among that happy band, moving from this land of grace-assisted living to God's land of unmerited loving. And there is good reason for my hope. It is found in the truth expressed by Augustine long ago:

We are on our way to see the Christ who is God and the Christ who shares our humanity is the way through which we are going. We are going to him and we are going through him. Why then should any of us fear becoming lost? (*Sermon 123*, 1.3)

NOTES

1. The current teaching of the Catholic Church (as outlined in the official *Catechism of the Catholic Church*) would seem to agree with this list of the "saved." After stating that "Believing Jesus Christ and in the One who sent him for our salvation is necessary for obtaining that salvation" *(#161)*, it adds later on that

> Those who through no fault of their own, do not know the Gospel of Christ or his Church, but who nevertheless seek God with a sincere heart, and, moved by grace try in their actions to do his will as they know it through the dictates of their conscience . . . those too may achieve eternal salvation. *(#847)*

This statement does not address the salvation of those who are unable because of age or disability to make conscious decisions for or against God. At least the suggestion of God's saving will for such poor souls is implied in the statement regarding infants dying without baptism:

> As regards children who have died without baptism, the Church can only entrust them to the mercy of God. Indeed, the great mercy of God who desires that all men should be saved and Jesus's tenderness toward children which caused him to say: "let the children come to me, do not hinder them (Mark 10:14; 1 Tim 2:4), allows us to hope that there is a way of salvation for children who have died without Baptism. *(#1261)*

What these texts seem to conclude is that:

1. Those believing and baptized in Jesus Christ who do not turn their back on God at the end of their lives will be saved.
2. Those who without their fault do not possess that faith but who try to follow the will of God as this is revealed through their conscience will also be saved.
3. God's mercy allows us to hope that those who are innocent, that is unable to make a decision for or against God, will also be taken care of by the good God.

The ambivalence of these last statements is simply a humble admission that how God works with the "good living pagan" or those innocents incapable of personal sin remains a mystery.

2. John Sachs gives the following summary of the current views of Catholic theologians writing about heaven and hell (John R. Sachs, S.J., "Current Eschatology: Universal Salvation and the Problem of Hell," *Theological Studies* [June 1991] 233–41):

1. Because human beings are free, they are able to reject God. Therefore hell is a real possibility.
2. Though final damnation remains a possibility with which every individual must reckon, neither Scripture nor Church teaching claims that anyone in fact has been or will be finally lost.
3. Certain knowledge about the final outcome of judgment for individuals is impossible, but because of Christ's victory over sin and death, we may and must hope that all men and women will in fact be saved.

Epilogue:
The Caterpillar and the Butterfly

One of my favorite places in all the world is a bench high above the sea just north of Hampton Beach on the New Hampshire coast. During my years teaching in New England, I used to go there on Saturday just to sit watching the quiet sea sliding past under a sky that was the bluest of the blue. I was cooled by the gentle ocean breeze and all the world seemed bright and fresh and clean. I was at peace.

There was a low hedge bordering the path where I sat, and in season it burst forth in tiny red and blue flowers that added to the colors of the day. Also in season it was populated by hundreds of regal Monarch butterflies who flitted from blossom to blossom gathering nourishment for their long journey beyond the sea.

The thought struck me that the story of their lives was something like the story of the life of every human being. All butterflies begin their existence in the darkness of a tiny egg. They are alive but undeveloped with little awareness of the world in which they are growing. Externally all seem the same (perhaps hinting at the nature they all share in common), but internally the forces are already at work that will define them as unique individuals.

Finally bursting from its egg, the butterfly enters the next stage of its life as a caterpillar. Even in their days of infancy some are very attractively clothed in multi-colored coats. Others are just dull hairy bugs. Some have poisons in their skin to protect them from predators. Others depend on camouflage, hiding among the leaves and branches of their environment lest they be "squashed" by passing giants. Despite their apparent fragility they are in fact "eating machines" creating havoc on the uncomplaining trees and bushes that support them.

As life goes on, the caterpillar sheds its skin many times as it grows larger and larger, putting off the meekness of youth to take on the grandeur of maturity. Finally, in its last days it wraps itself in its last well-worn skin and becomes a chrysalis, a being quite unlike its former self, a silent self-made cocoon swinging gently in the breeze, reaping now the effects of the good and bad of its caterpillar days. It is a precarious existence and some do not survive too long, but those that do gradually grow to maturity and finally spring forth as glorious butterflies.

All butterflies have their own unique beauty but the Monarch is especially well-named. It has the colors and size of butterfly royalty. Though delicate, its great wings carry it far and wide. Surviving its nondescript existence as an egg, its humdrum existence as a caterpillar, its quiet sleep as a chrysalis, it at last springs forth as a majestic full-formed butterfly.

As a caterpillar the Monarch was limited to this little bush, this little leaf, this little piece of earth, but now in its day of resurrection it has a glorious body and ebullient spirit that enables it to fly freely, spreading its beauty to lands far beyond the sea. Supported by God's favoring breezes the Monarch seems able to fly even to heaven itself.

The story of the caterpillar and the butterfly reminds me of where I have come from, where I am now, and where I am going. I, too, started as a simple egg, a living thing of no apparent importance that was slowly developing into a form that could deal with the world outside. Bursting from the womb, I began my career as an eating machine, in the early years thinking (if I thought at all) of nothing beyond the next meal and a safe place to rest. I struggled through this new world crawling, munching whatever delicacy came my way. I was not unhappy because in my baby days I knew of no other life.

As I grew I began to shed my skin. I literally "got too big for my britches" and successively burst from infancy into childhood and then maturity, growing bigger and bigger. As I grew, I puffed myself up and painted myself with degrees and titles to fend off those who might threaten me. Of course, one difference between myself and the caterpillar is that, besides eating and growing and wandering about on the leaf where fate had placed me, I sought another to love. I said to myself: "My life will become even more complete if I can find someone like myself who will truly *like* my 'self' and perhaps even love me."

Eventually all of the plans and dreams of youth began to dim. I felt the winter coming on. I realized that what I would be here on earth could be nothing more than "what I was." Further development was arrested by my gradual deterioration as I begin to wrap myself in my last somewhat scarred and wrinkled skin.

When death comes, I will enter my own "chrysalis" state, gently swinging to and fro in the place reserved for me by my past actions. I will then be in a state called "purgatory," still alive but no longer in the old body that I had gotten used to over the years. I will be a living spirit waiting in my cocoon for resurrection.

My Christian faith tells me that the day of my resurrection will come, a day when I will burst out of the silence of my tomb with a new body quite unlike the body of my "caterpillar" days in this Hospice. I will burst forth with a new body and an enlivened spirit that will send me into the heavens to enjoy the bracing air and gentle breezes of the land where God dwells.

As I watch my friends the Monarch butterflies departing happily to lands unknown, excitedly flying this way and that in a joyous dance with their friends, going higher and higher until finally disappearing from the land where caterpillars crawl, I think of the promises made by Jesus that someday I will fly even higher into a land beyond time, a land where finally and forever I will be at home with my flesh and blood: Jesus Christ the Lord.

Warmed by the afternoon sun as I sit on my little bench by the sea, I think of such things and ask myself: "Why is it that now I sometimes get so afraid of my future, a time when I will be able to fly in the heavens for all eternity?" Perhaps it is because now in my "caterpillar" days I have a form of agoraphobia, a fear of open spaces. I know what there is here on earth, but what waits for me in the unlimited space and time beyond the doors of this Hospice is still a mystery. I have heard stories about it but I really don't know. Perhaps all I can do just now is to hold onto my belief that there is a loving God with infinite powers who will take care of things.

In any case, I should not be ashamed of being afraid. I suspect that even the lowly caterpillar would be a bit afraid if it ever learned of the unimaginable "butterfly" days that lay ahead.